PIRATE CUISINE

A Children's Cookbook

Ivan Kushnir

Pirate Cuisine: A Children's Cookbook. - 2025.

Pirate Cuisine — the treasure children have been waiting for!
This is not just a cookbook — it's a pirate adventure on every page, where each recipe becomes a journey filled with the scent of spices, tales of sea rogues, and the spirit of distant shores.

Here's why this book is, without exaggeration, a hit:
Each region — the Caribbean, Barbary Coast, Somalia, Malabar, the China Sea, England, Norway — has its own cuisine, pirates, dishes, and legends.
Vivid titles spark emotion: "Fried Fish with Lime and Mango — a Tasty Treasure," "Rum-Scented Ice Cream — a Cold Treasure," "Chebakia — Sweet Rose Blossoms."
Child-friendly language and humor blend beautifully with authenticity and educational content.
Over 90 recipes! All with a pirate twist — simple, exotic, and made with local ingredients.
It's a perfect gift and an exciting learning tool.

It's easy to imagine children grabbing this book and "playing pirates," cooking up dishes from a new sea each day.
They're not just learning to cook — they're traveling the world.
Yes! Kids have been waiting for a book like this. And not only kids.

https://books-6-12.blogspot.com/

ISBN: 9798286202676

Contents

10 Pirate Stories with a Hint of Spices

1. Captain Anise and the Golden Fish Soup.

Once upon a time in the Bay of Spicy Pepper, there lived the famous Captain Anise, who could cook a soup that glowed in the dark! His secret ingredient was a goldfish with luminescent scales. Captain added coconut milk, hot pepper, and sea mint to the broth. It is said that one spoonful of this soup gave the strength to sail against the current... even to a ship!

2. Mary Papaya and Her Flying Pancakes.

Pirate Mary Papaya was famous for her banana pancakes that could jump out of the pan. She cooked them on a special tropical stone and used dried coconut instead of flour. Once, her pancakes jumped right into the arms of enemy sailors — and instead of a fight, they offered to exchange recipes!

3. Sally Sardine and the Mystery of the Black Sauce.

When Sally Sardine's ship got stuck in a storm, she invented a new dish from fish and a mysterious black sauce made from caramelized bananas and coconut shell charcoal. The aroma was so enticing that sharks swam nearby not to attack, but to ask for more!

4. Dough Johnny and the Pirate Dragon Bread.

Baker Dough Johnny bakes bread that makes a "grrr!" sound when sliced. He mixes sea salt, pineapple juice, and spices from the island of Jamaica. One loaf was so hot that it warmed an entire deck during a storm. It was called "Dragon Bread" — it warms the heart of every pirate.

5. Molly Mango and the Song of Lime Sorbet.

Pirate Molly had a magical mango and lime sorbet that sang as it melted. Pirate children eagerly awaited the evening to hear its song — it led to dreamy sleep and adventures in sweet tropical dreams. Even the grumpiest captains became kinder after a spoonful of this ice cream.

6. Rum Jack and the Dancing Pudding.

Although Jack never drank rum, he added a rum flavor to his pudding. His dessert would start to tremble and "dance" on the plate as soon as it heard music! Once, the pudding got so carried away with dancing that it jumped overboard — a dolphin caught it and became the new pudding supplier on Dessert Island.

7. Greta Pumpkin and Her Cunning Gratin.

Greta cooked pumpkin gratin with seaweed that changed flavor depending on the eater's mood. Happy? — Sweet. Sad? — Mildly salty. Angry? — Oh, fiery hot! Her dish taught pirates to understand their emotions through taste.

8. Shrimp Larry and His Jumping Barbecue.

Larry grilled shrimp so that they jumped around the pan from the spices. He seasoned them with passion fruit juice, garlic, and roasted pineapple powder. Once, his shrimp helped him escape from an enemy ship — he threw them on the deck, and they jumped, creating chaos!

9. Lady Ginger and the Reef Tea Ritual.

Lady Ginger brewed ginger-cinnamon tea that even a shark could drink. Every Sunday, she held tea ceremonies right on the coral reef. Even sea turtles came — for the sweet cane candy with tea. It is said that her tea could melt the ice in the heart of the fiercest captain.

10. Child Captain Chili and the Cookie with a Treasure Inside.

Little Captain Chili bakes cookies with secrets. Inside each one is a miniature map, a clue, or a pirate word. The cookies are made with ginger, cocoa, sea salt, and a hope for adventure. They are given to pirate children who are just beginning their culinary journey on the sea of imagination!

Caribbean Pirates

1. Breakfast in the Bay: Banana Pancakes with a Tropical Twist.

Pirates started their day not with heavy meals, but with a light, energetic breakfast. Banana pancakes, similar to regular pancakes, were popular due to the availability of ripe bananas. They were fried in coconut oil and served with sugarcane syrup or mango puree. Often, a piece of salted herring or a fried coconut patty was on the table — energy for a day full of adventures!

2. Fish Soup "Run Down": A Fragrant Culinary Treasure.

For lunch, pirates loved thick, hearty soups. One of the most popular was "Run Down" — a fish stew in coconut milk with sweet potatoes, yams, green onions, garlic, and Scotch bonnet peppers. The fish was caught right from the ship and cooked immediately — freshness was the key to flavor. This soup was considered a true elixir of strength and vigor, especially after long night watches.

3. Main Course: "Escovitch Fish" with a Jamaican Character.

For dinner, pirates often enjoyed the famous "Escovitch Fish" — marinated, fried fish (usually red snapper) with a hot vegetable sauce. Onions, carrots, sweet peppers, spices, and vinegar created a fiery-sweet sauce that covered the hot fish. The dish was served cold or warm, often with fried plantains or coconut rice.

4. Sides: Coconut Rice and Fried Plantains.

Coconut rice with beans is a true Caribbean signature. It was cooked in coconut milk with garlic, thyme, and spices. Plantains — similar to bananas but larger — were fried over coals or in a pan until golden brown. They added a sweet-salty accent to the main fish dishes and paired wonderfully with spicy sauces.

5. Captain's Snack: "Conch Fritters" from the Depths of the Sea.

Conch shells were not only decorative but also a source of delicacy. The conch meat was minced, mixed with onions, garlic, peppers, herbs, and fried into balls — "Conch Fritters." They were served with a spicy sauce or lime juice. This was a favorite snack of captains before dinner — nutritious and piquant.

6. **Beverages: Rum Legends and Children's Alternatives.**

Adult pirates loved rum, but for children or during the heat, they made "Sorrel" — a hibiscus drink with ginger, cinnamon, and nutmeg. It was served chilled, and the aroma filled the deck. Another popular drink was coconut water — straight from a green coconut, refreshing and slightly sweet.

7. **Desserts: Coconut Sweets from Sandy Shores.**

For dessert, pirates loved "Toto" — a dense coconut cake with nutmeg, cinnamon, and brown sugar. It was baked over a fire or in a clay oven on the shore. Another popular treat was "Guava Duff" — a roll with guava jam. Both desserts symbolized the tropical abundance of the islands.

8. **The Tradition of Communal Dinner — The Soul of the Pirate Crew.**

Pirates did not eat alone. Dinner was an important part of their lives — they gathered together, shared trophies and stories. Cooks often improvised with the catch — sometimes adding sea urchins, shrimp, or even seaweed to the fish. It was a time for laughter, songs, and dances to the sound of drums.

9. **Food as Part of Survival: Salting and Smoking.**

Pirates had to preserve food for a long time. Fish was often salted or smoked to prevent spoilage in the tropical climate. Salted cod — "Saltfish" — was a versatile ingredient: it was added to soups, fried with eggs, or made into patties. This method of food preservation helped them survive even in the most remote bays.

10. **The Taste of the Caribbean — More Than Just Food, It's a Story.**

The cuisine of Caribbean pirates is a mosaic of cultures: African, European, Indigenous, and Asian influences. It was formed at the crossroads of sea routes, where every spice, vegetable, or fish had its own story. These dishes are not just a tasty adventure but a window into the past, to times when even a simple soup was a treasure on a deserted island.

The cuisine of Caribbean pirates is more than just food. It is a culture of survival, creativity, and community. It taught the value of fresh ingredients, the combination of simple and delicious, and the celebration of every meal as an event

Tasting these dishes, we travel back in time — to a place where every meal was a little adventure.

Fried Fish with Lime and Mango: A Delicious Treasure from the Heart of the Caribbean!

1. Hello, young pirate! Let's prepare for a culinary raid!

The sails are unfurled, and the kitchen stove is our ship! Today, we will prepare a true pirate dish — fried fish with lime and mango, just as the sea wolves loved it in the Caribbean. But before we start, don't forget: working in the galley (that's what they call the kitchen on a ship) must be done safely! So ask an adult to be your sailor-helper. Ready? Let's go on a culinary boarding!

2. Gathering ingredients — treasures from a tropical island.

Here's what you'll need:
— 2 fillets of white fish (such as tilapia or dorado)
— 1 ripe mango
— 1 lime
— a little olive oil
— salt and black pepper
— a clove of garlic
— a pinch of paprika (not spicy!)
— a bit of greens (cilantro or parsley)

Found all the ingredients in your holds? Excellent!

3. Preparing the fish — how to clean it without a saber.

Is the fillet ready? Then just rinse it with water and pat it dry with a napkin. If there are still bones in the fish, that's a job for the adult helper. Meanwhile, you are the captain of spices! Salt and pepper the fish, add a little paprika. Rub it with a clove of garlic (but wash your hands afterward — garlic is strong, like rum!)

4. Magical lime marinade.

Cut the lime in half and squeeze the juice onto the fish. This will give it freshness, like ocean spray. Leave the fish in this juice for 10 minutes. This is called marinating. Pirates didn't have refrigerators, but they knew citrus keeps food fresh!

5. Preparing mango — the sweet treasure of the tropics.

Peel the mango (ask for help if needed — it's as slippery as an eel!) and cut it into cubes. You can add the mango raw to the fish, or fry it a little in a pan for a caramel flavor. Oh, what an aroma!

6. The galley in action — frying the fillet in a pan.

Pour a little oil into the pan and ask an adult to turn on the stove. When the oil is hot, place the fish. Be careful! The fish fries for 2-3 minutes on each side. It will become golden, like treasure in the sun. Don't flip it often, so it doesn't break apart!

7. Pirate decoration — tropical salsa!

Mix the chopped mango with finely chopped greens and a few drops of lime juice. This is pirate salsa — fresh, aromatic, perfect for fish. You can add a little pepper if you're as brave as Jack Sparrow!

8. Serving — how to present it to impress the captains.

Place the fillet on a plate, top it with salsa. Garnish with lime slices and greens. If you want, add a little rice or mashed potatoes on the side — it will be a real pirate feast!

9. **Secrets of kitchen pirates.**
— Always wash your hands before starting to cook.
— The juiciness of the fish is preserved if it's not overcooked.
— Lime can be replaced with lemon, but lime is more tropical!
— Mango should be soft and fragrant, then it's sweet.

10. **Careful, sailor!**

The pan is as hot as the Caribbean sun! Never touch it with bare hands. Use a kitchen spatula. Don't leave the stove unattended — even the best pirates don't abandon their dish!

And here it is — fried fish with lime and mango is ready!

Tasting it, you'll feel the breath of the sea, the song of seagulls, and tropical freshness. It's not just food — it's a part of Caribbean culture, where every spice has a story, and every dish is its own treasure. Bon appétit, captain! The next culinary adventure is already waiting on the horizon!

Coconut Rice with Shrimp: Tropical Gold on a Plate!

1. **Young pirate, today we are cooking tropical gold!**

When pirates returned to the Caribbean after long journeys, they dreamed of something warm, fragrant, and hearty. And that's when coconut rice with shrimp was prepared in the galley — a dish that smells of adventure, the sea, and palm trees! So put on your apron, gather the crew, and let's set sail on a culinary voyage!

2. **Your list of tropical treasures — ingredients.**

Gather provisions for the recipe:
— 1 cup of long-grain rice (preferably jasmine)
— 200 ml of coconut milk (from a can)
— 1/2 cup of water
— 200 g of peeled shrimp
— 1 small onion
— 1 clove of garlic
— a bit of oil (preferably coconut or olive)
— salt, pepper
— a pinch of turmeric or curry (for color, like pirate gold!)
— a slice of lime and fresh herbs for garnish

3. **Prepare the rice — the base of our dish.**

Rinse the rice in a bowl several times until the water is clear — this will make it fluffy. Then ask an adult to place a pot on the stove. Pour in the coconut milk and water, add the rice, a bit of salt, and a pinch of turmeric. When the liquid boils, reduce the heat to a minimum and cover with a lid. Cook for 15-18 minutes until the rice absorbs all the liquid. The whole galley will smell like a coconut bay!

4. **While the rice is cooking — prepare the spicy shrimp.**

Heat a bit of oil in a pan. Finely chop the garlic and onion. Ask an adult to help sauté them until they are soft. Then add the shrimp, a bit of salt, and pepper. Sauté them for 3-4 minutes — no longer, or they will become as tough as an old pirate boot sole!

5. **The secret of aroma — the combination of spices.**

If you want to add a bit of spiciness, sprinkle a pinch of curry or paprika on the shrimp. You can also grate a bit of lime zest — only the yellow part, as the white is bitter. This is the true secret of tropical aroma, known only to the ship's cook of the "Black Pearl"!

6. **Combine the treasures: shrimp meet rice.**

When the rice is ready, gently mix it with a fork (not a spoon, to keep it from sticking!). Add the sautéed shrimp. If you like, you can serve the shrimp separately on top — it looks like treasures laid out on the sand!

7. **Serving on a pirate's plate.**

Place a portion of rice on a plate, with a few shrimp on top. Garnish with green leaves and a slice of lime. You can serve it with thin slices of pineapple or mango on the side — pirates loved to combine salty and sweet. Arrr!

8. **Old sea wolf's tips:**
— Always taste the coconut milk before using — it should be fresh and aromatic.
— If the shrimp are frozen, thaw them in cold water, not in the microwave.
— For a brighter color, add a pinch of saffron — but know, it's more expensive than pirate doubloons!

9. **Be careful in the galley!**

The pan and pot are hot — stay away from the fire without adults. Always use a towel or potholder. If something spills, clean it up immediately, or you might slip like on a wet deck during a storm!

10. **Time to feast under the Caribbean sun!**

Sit down with friends or family, serve the dish on a palm leaf napkin or in a coconut bowl — and imagine yourself on a tropical island. This aromatic rice and shrimp are not just food; it's part of the pirate legacy that can be cooked at home with just a bit of imagination and desire!

That's it, captain!

You've prepared a dish that would be proudly served at a banquet in Tortuga Bay. The taste of the Caribbean — sweet, spicy, with notes of adventure. Now you're not just a cabin boy, but a true pirate cook! To new culinary journeys!

Fish Soup "Run Down": Caribbean Storm in a Bowl!

1. **Hello, young chef of the seven seas!**

Today we will cook a real Caribbean dish — fish soup "Run Down". This dish was prepared on the shores of Jamaica when pirates anchored in tropical bays. The soup turns out to be rich, aromatic, and slightly spicy — perfect for warming up after a sea storm! But it should be cooked carefully, so invite an adult helper and let's start our culinary raid!

2. **Ingredients — your culinary treasure.**

What you need to take from the holds:
— 300 g of white fish fillet (such as tilapia, hake, or dorado)
— 1 cup of coconut milk
— 1 small onion
— 1 tomato
— 1 clove of garlic
— 1 small sweet pepper
— 1 small piece of green onion or parsley
— salt, pepper, a pinch of thyme (dried or fresh)
— a piece of chili pepper (optional, only for brave captains!)

3. **Preparation: deck washing and fish cleaning.**

The fish needs to be well rinsed and checked for bones (an adult helmsman should do this). Then cut the fillet into large pieces — they should hold their shape during cooking. Salt and pepper them, and add a little thyme. Let it marinate for a few minutes — this is called "marinating".

4. **Coconut cauldron: the foundation of everything.**

Pour a cup of coconut milk into a deep pot. This will be our magical base — thick, slightly sweet, tropical. Place the pot on the stove over medium heat. Ask an adult to be nearby — coconut milk loves to escape!

5. **Adding colors: vegetables on the deck!**

Dice the tomato, slice the onion into half rings, mince the garlic, and cut the pepper into strips.

If adding chili — only a small piece, and only with an adult's permission. Add everything to the pot with the coconut milk. Cook for 5 minutes — the aroma will spread like a pirate flag signal!

6. **Place the fish in the magical coconut ocean.**

Carefully lower the pieces of fish into the boiling milk with vegetables. Cover with a lid and let it cook for 10-12 minutes on low heat. Do not stir intensively — the fish is delicate, like a sail in calm weather.

7. **Secret pirate trick: "run down" means to reduce!**

This soup needs to be reduced a bit, meaning let the coconut milk become thicker. If the liquid is too thin — cook for another 5 minutes uncovered. This way, the soup will resemble a sauce and be just perfect for bread or rice!

8. **The final touch: greens and flavor balance.**

At the end, add chopped greens (parsley or green onion), a pinch of salt, pepper, and lime juice if desired. Remove the pot from the heat. The smell is like after rain on a tropical island!

9. **Pirate-style serving.**

Pour the soup into a deep bowl, serve with pieces of fresh bread, baked bananas, or fluffy rice. You can eat it with a spoon or even with a bread "spoon", as the pirates did. Don't forget a napkin — tropical dishes love to spread!

10. **Tips from the captain-chef:**

— Don't add too much chili — this is not a duel, but dinner!
— If you don't have coconut milk — you can make it yourself: pour 2 tablespoons of shavings with 1 cup of hot water, infuse, and strain.
— "Run Down" soup can also be made with shrimp or even vegetables — the main thing is to have the soul of the Caribbean!
So, young sailor, your "Run Down" is ready!

You have just recreated a real pirate recipe that once saved sailors from hunger during a storm.

This dish is warm, hearty, aromatic, like a cozy bay after a storm. Eat boldly, with imagination, and don't be afraid of culinary waves! To a new adventure — full speed ahead!

Grilled Perch with Pineapples: Dinner for a Pirate King!

1. **Young pirate, today we grill perch — a treasure from the deep waters!**

This dish is a true culinary masterpiece of the Caribbean Sea. Pirates loved to combine the sea and the tropics, so grilled fish with sweet pineapple pieces was a favorite dish at pirate feasts. In this episode, you'll learn how to prepare grilled perch with pineapples — simple, delicious, and a bit adventurous!

2. **Prepare the ingredients — your culinary trophies:**

— 1 whole perch (cleaned, descaled; or 2 fillets)
— 3 slices of pineapple (fresh or canned, without syrup)
— 2 tablespoons of olive oil
— juice of half a lime
— a clove of garlic
— a pinch of salt and pepper
— fresh herbs (such as cilantro or parsley)
— a pinch of paprika or turmeric (for color, like in pirate chests!)

3. **Clean and prepare the fish — with respect for the ocean depths.**

If the fish is whole, have an adult remove the head, tail, and fins. Rinse the fish under water, pat dry with a towel. If you have fillets — great, proceed to the marinade. The main thing is to ensure there are no bones left in the fish (an adult helper checks this!)

4. **Pirate marinade — as simple as laying out a treasure map.**

In a bowl, mix lime juice, oil, finely chopped garlic, salt, pepper, and a pinch of paprika. Place the fish in this marinade. Let it marinate for 10–15 minutes — during this time, it absorbs the aroma of the tropics and adventure!

5. **Prepare the pineapple — the sweet ally of the perch.**

Cut the pineapple into rings or halves. If it's fresh — great! If from a can — drain the liquid. Grilled pineapple is like the sun on the deck, sweet, warm, and with a caramel crust. We will grill it alongside the fish.

6. **Time to grill — the pirate culinary battle begins!**

If you have a home electric grill — great. If a grill pan — that works too! Let an adult turn on the grill or stove and grease the surface with oil. When hot — place the fish. Grill for 3–4 minutes on each side (fillets — a bit less). Then place the pineapple and grill until golden brown.

7. **Vigilance — the main virtue in the galley.**

The pan is like a hot cannonball, don't touch it without a mitt. Ask an adult to flip the fish with a spatula. Don't grill too long — the fish will become dry, like a sail in the heat. Pineapple is quick, 1–2 minutes on each side is enough.

8. **Culinary decoration — make the plate a treasure map!**

Place the fish on a large plate, with pineapple pieces on top or on the side. Garnish with herbs and drops of lime juice. You can even place a lemon slice in the shape of the sun or arrange pineapple rings like an island!

9. **Pirate tips to preserve your fame:**

— Don't be afraid to experiment: you can add a bit of honey to the marinade if you like it sweeter.
— If you want more sauce — mix some yogurt, lime juice, and herbs — it will be fresh!
— Perch is not the only hero. You can also prepare dorado, tilapia, or trout in the same way.

10. **Hooray, captain! Your grilled perch is ready!**

Enjoy the dish, imagining you're sitting on a shore with golden sand, and behind you is a ship with your flag. This is not just a meal — it's a celebration of pirate bravery, friendship, and the power of culinary imagination!

Landing completed: fish caught, pineapples gathered, dinner prepared!

Caribbean cuisine teaches us to combine different flavors — just as pirates combined different cultures. And now you are part of this culinary legend. To a new delicious expedition, captain!

Grilled Shark with Spicy Sauce: A Dish for the Bravest Captains!

1. Hello, young pirate! Get ready for a culinary duel with a shark!

In the Caribbean seas, sharks commanded respect even from the bravest pirates. But not all sharks are scary — some ended up on the pirate grill! Today, we will prepare pieces of shark fillet with a spicy sauce. Don't be afraid — cooking this dish is easier than storming a ship! But be careful — there are spices, fire, and an aroma that will awaken even a sleeping kraken!

2. Treasures in the hold — here's what you'll need:

— 2 pieces of shark fillet (or another firm fish: tuna, swordfish)
— juice of 1 lime
— 1 tbsp olive oil
— salt, black pepper
— a pinch of paprika or turmeric
— for the sauce: 1 small chili (or a pinch of ground), 1 clove of garlic, 1 tbsp ketchup, 1 tsp honey, a bit of lime juice

3. Preparing the fish — how to tame a sea predator.

The shark fillet should be boneless. It's firm, meaty, and doesn't fall apart when grilled — perfect for a pirate grill! Rinse the fish, pat dry with a paper towel, and cut into serving pieces. Then rub with salt, pepper, paprika, and lime juice. Let it stand for 10 minutes in a cool place — like a sailor before a battle.

4. **Preparing the pirate sauce — hellish and sweet at the same time!**

Mix minced garlic, ketchup, a bit of chili, honey, and lime juice in a small bowl. Stir well with a spoon. If you like it spicy — add more chili. If not — leave just the aroma, without the fire. This sauce is like a pirate surprise: sweet at first, hot at the end!

5. **To battle, captain! The grill is hot!**

Ask an adult helper to heat up the electric grill or grill pan. Grease the surface with oil. When hot — place the shark fillet. Grill for 3–4 minutes on each side. The shark should not be raw inside, but don't overcook it either!

6. **Watch your fish like a captain watches his schooner during a storm.**

Don't flip the fish back and forth on the grill — carefully turn it once when you see a delicious golden crust forming on the bottom. Use a spatula or tongs for this (and trust only adults with these "pirate tools"!)

7. **Coat the fish — with a sauce that conquered the Caribbean!**

After both sides of the fish are grilled, coat it with our sauce and leave it for another minute on the grill so the sauce thickens a bit and sticks like a ship to reefs. The aroma will be such that you'll want to shout "Arrr!"

8. **Serving on the deck — like a feast in Tortuga!**

Place the shark fillet on a plate, alongside lime slices, some greens, rice or potatoes, and pieces of pineapple or mango — just as pirates loved after long journeys. You can even decorate the dish with a small flag with a skull — culinary piracy is allowed!

9. **Sea advice from Captain Jeremy Sharp-Tongue:**

— It's better to apply the sauce at the end so it doesn't burn.
— If there's no shark — no problem. Use any firm fish.
— Don't overcook the fillet: it's better to slightly undercook and let it "finish" on the plate.
— Always wash your hands after working with chili — and don't scratch your nose or eyes (pirates warned!)

10. **Dinner is ready, young sailor! You've conquered the culinary sea!**

This dish is like a real pirate battle: a bit of fire, lots of flavor, and victory in every bite. You've learned not only to cook but also to skillfully command in the kitchen. The next adventure is already calling — take a spoon instead of a sword and set off on delicious sea voyages!

Pirate wisdom: spicy is not always scary if you hold the sauce in your hands!

Grilled shark with spicy sauce is like an adventure in a stormy sea. And now you are not just a young sailor, but a true pirate-chef, respected on all culinary islands!

Crab Salad with Papaya: A Light Dish for Pirates Under the Sails!

1. **Young pirate, today we are in the tropics — preparing a salad for true sea gourmets!**

In the hot Caribbean, when the sun blazes like a hot pan, pirates didn't always want heavy meals. And then, a fresh, vibrant, aromatic crab salad with papaya appeared in the galley — perfect for a deck picnic! This salad is a true treasure from the sea and tropics, full of colors, flavors, and unexpected combinations.

2. **Gathering ingredients — your culinary trophies from Treasure Island:**

— 150 g of cooked crab meat (can be replaced with crab sticks if real crab is not in the hold)
— 1 ripe papaya
— 1/2 cucumber
— juice of half a lime
— 1 teaspoon of honey
— a little olive oil
— salt, pepper
— a few lettuce or spinach leaves
— fresh herbs (cilantro or parsley)

3. **Preparing the crab — without claws, but with respect!**

Cut the crab meat or sticks into small pieces. If it's real crab, ask an adult to help extract the meat from the shells — those claws aren't so simple! Important: the meat should be boneless or cartilage-free to not spoil the fun dinner.

4. **Tropical papaya — sweet, juicy, and very pirate-like!**

Peel the papaya, remove the seeds (they're black and slimy, like pearls from sea oysters!), and cut the flesh into cubes. If the papaya is ripe, it will be soft, bright, and smell like a tropical garden. If there's no papaya, you can use mango or pineapple.

5. **Cucumber — coolness after battling the sun.**

Cut the cucumber into half-moons or thin strips. The cucumber will add crunch to the salad — like snow at the South Pole if pirates ever sailed there. And it pairs wonderfully with sweet papaya!

6. **Mixing the sauce — a culinary elixir from the tropics.**

In a small bowl, mix lime juice, a spoonful of honey, a little oil, a pinch of salt, and pepper. Mix well with a spoon or whisk — the sauce should be sweet and sour, like pirate songs after a successful boarding!

7. **Time to mix the ingredients — the kitchen captain in action!**

In a large bowl, combine papaya, crab meat, cucumber, and herbs. Add the sauce and gently mix with a spoon or gloved hands. You can serve the salad on lettuce leaves — like on a tropical plate, straight from palm leaves!

8. **Serving — like at a feast in Tortuga Bay!**

Arrange the salad in deep bowls or shells (pirate style!), top with herb leaves and a slice of lime. If you wish, add some roasted nuts or pomegranate seeds. It will look like a true culinary treasure!

9. **Culinary secrets from veteran pirates:**
— If you want more tropical flavor, add a few pieces of mango or pineapple rings.
— You can use canned papaya, but fresh is better.
— Crab sticks should be slightly chilled before preparation — the taste will be fresher.

10. **Safety tips on the culinary ship:**
— Papaya is slippery, so cut it carefully, preferably on a board with rubber feet.
— Always wash your hands after working with fish products.
— A knife is not a pirate sword! Use it carefully and under the supervision of an adult helper.

That's it, captain! Crab salad with papaya is ready to serve!

This light, aromatic, vibrant salad will not only refresh you in the heat but also remind you of those distant islands where pirates sang, celebrated, and shared food around the fire. Now you are also part of this culinary legend. To new tropical adventures, young pirate!

Banana Donuts: A Sweet Treasure from a Tropical Island!

1. **Yo-ho-ho, Captain! Today we fry donuts for the entire crew!**

After a long voyage, even the bravest pirates dream of something sweet. In the Caribbean, where bananas grow at every turn, culinary sailors invented banana donuts — fluffy, fragrant, sweet, and golden like pirate doubloons! Prepare the captain's apron — and we're off on a sweet adventure!

2. Overview of tropical ingredients — your treasure chest:
— 2 ripe bananas (soft, with spots — just right!)
— 1 egg
— 3 tbsp sugar
— 1/2 cup milk
— 1 cup flour
— 1 tsp baking powder
— a pinch of salt
— a bit of cinnamon (optional — like the aroma from a rum barrel!)
— oil for frying (sunflower or coconut)
— powdered sugar for sprinkling

3. Mashing bananas — a fun task for the cabin boy!

Peel the bananas and place them in a deep bowl. Mash them with a fork, like a true pirate squeezes citrus for lime juice! The banana should turn into a puree — this will be the base of our dough.

4. Mixing the dough — a magical elixir of sweetness.

Add the egg, sugar, milk, and a pinch of salt to the banana puree. Mix well with a whisk or spoon. Then gradually add the flour with baking powder (and cinnamon, if you like), stirring until the dough resembles thick sour cream. If it drips slowly — perfect!

5. Frying — a culinary battle with fire (only under the watchful eye of the cook-helmsman)!

Pour oil into a deep frying pan or small cauldron to a height of 2–3 fingers. Ask an adult to heat it over medium heat. Check readiness: a drop of dough should immediately float and fry with bubbles.

6. Releasing banana "bombs" into the oily ocean!

Carefully scoop the dough with a teaspoon and place it in the hot oil. Fry for 1–2 minutes on each side until the donuts are golden, like pirate gold. Place them on paper towels to remove excess oil.

7. Vigilance in the galley — the key to a safe celebration!

The oil is hot, like midday sand! So never lean over the pan and don't drop the dough from a height. Work slowly, carefully, and most importantly — together with an adult who has permission to wear the kitchen captain's hat!

8. Time to decorate — donuts turn into culinary treasures!

When the donuts have cooled for a few minutes, sprinkle them with powdered sugar (you can use a sieve). This way, they will look as if they have just come down from a magical tropical tree, sprinkled with pirate dust of adventure!

9. Serving — worthy of a feast on the deck after a storm.

Arrange the banana donuts on a plate in a circle, place a small bowl of honey, chocolate, or fruit sauce in the center. And also — a few banana slices or berries on top. Beautiful, delicious, and fun!

10. Pirate tips for the young confectioner:
— If the dough is too runny, add a little more flour.
— Want a coconut flavor? Add a spoonful of grated coconut to the dough!
— Donuts are tasty even the next day if you hide them in a chest (container).

Hooray! Banana donuts are ready — and that means it's time to celebrate the victory over culinary waves!

These donuts are not just a dessert, they are a piece of a pirate's heart, memories of warm islands, songs under the stars, and adventures under sails. You have bravely endured the culinary boarding! To new flavors and sweet journeys, Captain!

Pirate Squid Skewers: Tropical Taste on a Stick!

1. Arrr, Captain! Time to grill squid — a delicacy from the depths of the Caribbean Sea!

Squids are not only excellent swimmers but also delicious food! Old pirates considered them a true delicacy, especially when pieces of squid were skewered on wooden sticks, grilled over a fire, and served with tropical sauce. Ready? Today you'll learn to make pirate squid skewers like a true sea cook!

2. Pirate Provision List — Searching for Culinary Treasures:
— 300 g of cleaned squid (bodies or rings)
— 1 tablespoon of olive or coconut oil
— juice of half a lime
— 1 clove of garlic
— a pinch of salt and black pepper
— a pinch of paprika or turmeric (for color and taste)
— a few wooden skewers (soak them in water for 10 minutes)
— optional: pieces of pepper, pineapple, or cherry tomatoes for the skewers

3. Preparing the Squid — No Ink, Just Taste!

If the squid is frozen, ask an adult to defrost it. Then rinse the squid under water. If they are bodies, cut them into strips or rings. If already cut, check for any inedible parts (cartilage or films). All set? Time to marinate!

4. Pirate Marinade — Taste of the Ocean and Spices.

In a bowl, mix oil, lime juice, minced garlic, salt, pepper, and paprika. Add the squid and mix well. Leave for 15 minutes while they soak up the aroma of adventure! It's like a short rest before the culinary battle!

5. Skewering Like True Pirates Skewered Fish on Harpoons!

Take the skewers and carefully thread the squid. You can alternate: a piece of squid, a cube of pepper, a slice of pineapple, a cherry tomato. This way, the skewers will be colorful and tasty! Don't skewer too tightly — each ingredient should have a bit of "air" around it.

6. Grill or Pan — Choose Your Culinary Ship!

Ask an adult to heat the grill or grill pan. Grease the surface with oil. When hot, place the skewers. Grill for 2–3 minutes on each side. Squid is very tender — if overcooked, they become tough, like the soles of an old pirate's boot!

7. Grilling — It's Not a Ship Assault. Precision is Needed!

Watch carefully: as soon as the squid turns white and slightly golden, they're ready. Remove the skewers onto a plate, carefully, don't burn yourself. Use tongs or a spatula. And remember — no fingers in the hot pan!

8. Serving on the Deck — Delicious as a Pirate Victory!

Place the skewers on a plate, garnish with greens and lime slices. You can serve with rice, vegetables, or sauce: for example, yogurt with garlic, or sweet-spicy with honey and chili. Looks like a feast in the treasure bay!

9. Tips from Old Squid, the Cook on the "Black Fish":

— If the squid was rubbery, you overcooked it. Next time — less heat, fewer minutes!
— Add pieces of tropical fruits — they "absorb" the heat and add flavors.
— If there's no grill, use an oven with a "grill" function or a regular pan.

10. Warning from the Galley Captain:

— Skewers are sharp! Carefully thread the ingredients, or entrust this to an adult.
— Hot oil and grill — only with the help of a senior sailor.
— After working with squid, wash your hands and board — these are the sea hygiene rules!

Wow, young sailor, you've made real pirate squid skewers!

This is not just a delicious dish — it's a journey to the Caribbean on a ship with sails, aromas of spices, and waves! With each piece, you discover a new culinary map. The next stop — a new island of taste. Until the next culinary boarding adventure, Captain!

Spicy Stewed Fish with Sweet Potatoes: A Caribbean Storm in the Pot!

1. Arrr, Captain! Today we are cooking a stormy fish dish straight from the tropics!

In the Caribbean Sea, after rain and adventures, pirates loved to warm up with hearty stewed fish with sweet potatoes — the sweet potatoes they found on the islands. This dish is warm, aromatic, and a bit spicy, just like a true pirate's character! Grab your wooden spoon and onward — to culinary boarding!

2. Stock up on provisions — a list of ingredients for a barrel of delicious treasure:
— 300 g fish fillet (such as tilapia, dorado, or hake)
— 1 medium sweet potato
— 1 carrot
— 1/2 onion
— 1 clove of garlic
— 1 tomato
— 1 tsp tomato paste (optional)
— 1/2 cup water or fish broth
— 1 tbsp oil
— a pinch of thyme, salt, pepper
— a piece of chili (optional, only for brave sailors!)

3. Preparing the fillet — fish to battle with sweet potatoes!

Rinse the fish, pat dry with a towel, and cut into large cubes. Salt, pepper, and sprinkle with a pinch of thyme. Let it marinate for 10 minutes — while other ingredients prepare for culinary sailing!

4. Peeling the vegetables — like pirates washing up before a feast!

Peel the sweet potato and carrot, cut into cubes or half-moons. Ask an adult for help, as sweet potatoes are as hard as a deck! Chop the tomato finely, and the onion and garlic even finer. The vegetables should come together in one pot — like pirates from different islands!

5. **Start cooking — drop anchor on the stove!**

Pour oil into a large pan or pot with a thick bottom. Heat (together with an adult), add onion and garlic. Fry until translucent — this will be an aromatic base, like a pirate signal fire in the fog.

6. **Add vegetables and spices — let it boil like the sea in a storm!**

Put the carrot, sweet potato, tomato, and tomato paste in the pan. Stir. Add a little salt, pepper, thyme, and (if desired) a bit of chili. Pour in half a cup of water or broth. Cover with a lid and stew for 10 minutes on low heat until the sweet potato becomes soft, like the captain's pillow.

7. **When it's time to add the fish — listen to the sea bell!**

When the vegetables are almost ready, carefully place the fish pieces on top of the vegetables. Cover again with a lid and stew for another 8–10 minutes until the fish becomes white and tender. Do not stir too much to avoid breaking the fillet — better gently "rock the ship" with a spoon!

8. **Time for final touches — add the aroma of victory!**

Taste it. If needed, add salt, lime juice, or a pinch of thyme. Sprinkle with fresh herbs (cilantro or parsley). It smells so good that even ghosts from pirate legends come out of the hold!

9. **Serving — like at a pirate feast!**

Place the stewed fish with vegetables in a deep plate. It can be served with rice or a slice of bread. Ideally — on a palm leaf or wooden board (for a pirate mood). Serve with a slice of lime and a pirate smile!

10. **Sea tips from Captain Red Kettle:**
— Do not overcook the fish — it will remain juicy.
— If there is no sweet potato, you can use regular potatoes, but the sweetness will be lost.
— The dish tastes even better the next day — if anything is left!
— Be careful with knives and the stove — this is a territory for working together with an adult cook-sailor!

That's all, Captain! Spicy stewed fish with sweet potatoes — your culinary victory!

This dish is not just a meal, but a real journey: from the deep sea waters to the sweet shores of the island of Batatos. With every spoonful, you discover new flavors, like a true explorer of the Caribbean! To new dishes and unforgettable culinary adventures, young sailor!

Sea Soup with Coconut and Greens: An Aromatic Wave with a Taste of Adventure!

1. **Arrr, young cook! Today we are cooking pirate sea soup — light, warm, and with the aroma of the tropics!**

This soup was a favorite dish of pirates on days when the sea was calm and the wind was warm. Hearty, tender, with a coconut flavor and green treasures, it warmed the hearts of even the most serious captains. Prepare a spoon instead of a saber — and let's set sail on a culinary wave!

2. **Provisions from the tropical market — treasures for the soup:**
— 150–200 g of fish fillet or seafood mix (mussels, shrimp, squid)
— 1 cup of coconut milk
— 2 cups of water or light vegetable broth
— 1 small potato (or sweet potato)
— 1 carrot
— 1/2 onion
— 1 clove of garlic
— a bunch of fresh greens (parsley, cilantro, or spinach)
— salt, pepper, a pinch of turmeric
— lime juice — optional

3. **Preparing the sea treasures — let's prepare the fish and vegetables!**

Rinse the fish or seafood mix under cold water. If you have shrimp, ask an adult to remove the shell. Cut the fish into small cubes. Peel and finely chop or cube the carrot, potato, and onion. This will be the base of our aromatic broth!

4. **Unfurl the sails of the soup adventure on the stove!**

Ask an adult to help place the pot on the stove. Pour in a little oil and sauté the onion with garlic until translucent — it's like the smoke from a pirate's fire, indicating that it will definitely be delicious!

5. **Vegetables in the pot — cooking the pirate base.**

Add the carrot and potato to the onion. Stir with a wooden spoon (pirates always used wooden utensils!). Pour in the water or broth. Add a pinch of salt and turmeric. Cover and cook for 10–12 minutes until the vegetables are as soft as a pillow on a pirate ship.

6. **Coconut milk — the secret tropical weapon!**

When the vegetables are soft, pour in the coconut milk. Stir — the soup will immediately turn white, like fog over the ocean. Then carefully add the fish or seafood. Cook for another 5–7 minutes, not allowing it to boil too much, so everything remains tender.

7. **Greens — an aromatic decoration from the island harbor!**

Chop the greens (cilantro, spinach, or parsley) and add to the soup 1–2 minutes before it's ready. You can add a few drops of lime juice — it will add freshness, like a sea breeze at dawn.

8. **Caution above all — even pirate cooks have rules!**
— The pot is hot! Use a potholder or ask an adult.
— Add the fish carefully to avoid scalding.
— Wash your hands and board after handling seafood.

9. **Serving — a treasure in a bowl!**

Pour the soup into a deep plate. You can garnish with greens or a small sail made of a stick and paper (place it on the edge of the plate). Serve with crispy croutons or a slice of coconut bread. It looks like a real captain's meal!

10. **Sea tips from Grandma Kokosina — the keeper of the recipe:**
— If you don't like fish, you can make the soup with just vegetables and coconut, it's delicious too!
— Turmeric adds color, but you need just a little.
— If you want a more tropical flavor, add a cube of pineapple at the end of cooking!

That's it, captain! Sea soup with coconut and greens — your culinary victory!

Now you're not just a cabin boy, but a true master of pirate soup. This dish is like sailing the Caribbean: aromatic, warm, and full of discoveries. To new flavors and sailing adventures, pirate cook!

Rum-Flavored Ice Cream: A Chilly Treasure from a Tropical Harbor!

(Alcohol-free — just a safe aroma for little pirates!)

1. **Arrr, Captain! Prepare your spoon and freezer — today we're making pirate ice cream with a rum flavor!**

After long journeys under the scorching Caribbean sun, pirates dreamed of something refreshing. And while real rum was only for adults, in pirate families, children were treated to ice cream with a spicy aroma reminiscent of rum — with vanilla, cinnamon, coconut, or raisins. This is the safe, aromatic version we will prepare!

2. **Supplies from the hold — ingredients for a frozen wonder:**

— 2 ripe bananas
— 1/2 cup of milk (or coconut milk)
— 1 tsp of vanilla sugar
— a pinch of cinnamon
— a few raisins (soaked in juice)
— 1 tsp of coconut flakes
— 1/2 tsp of non-alcoholic "rum" extract (if available) or a bit of vanilla and honey
— (optional) — a spoonful of yogurt or cream for creaminess

3. **Preparing the bananas — like peeling a tropical fruit under the stars!**

Peel the bananas and slice them into rounds. Place them in a container or bag and put them in the freezer for 2–3 hours (or overnight). This will be the base of your ice cream — natural, sugar-free, sweet, and tender!

4. **While the bananas freeze — prepare the "pirate treasures."**

Pour hot water or juice (like apple or pineapple) over the raisins for 10 minutes to soften them. Then drain the liquid. This is your "rum" note, but completely safe!

5. **Time to blend — the ice cream is almost on the horizon!**

In a blender bowl, place the frozen bananas, milk, vanilla, cinnamon, coconut flakes, raisins, and, if desired, a bit of yogurt. Blend until creamy — it will be tough at first, but in a minute, you'll have real magic — tender ice cream ready for adventure!

6. **Captain Sweet Sail's secret: ice cream is like a ship: it must reach its destination!**

If you want soft ice cream, you can eat it right away. If you prefer it firmer, place the mixture in a container and put it in the freezer for another hour. Remember: don't keep the ice cream too long — it will lose its tenderness, like a pirate without a compass!

7. **Serving — like a real treasure on a shell plate!**

Scoop the ice cream into bowls or coconut shells (if available), sprinkle with coconut flakes, and garnish with mint or a piece of pineapple. Want a real pirate effect? Stick in a stick and make ice cream popsicles!

8. **Caution, young sailor, even with ice cream!**

— Don't put your fingers in the blender while it's running — it's taboo even for the bravest pirates.
— Ask an adult to help with freezing and removing the ice cream from the container.
— Don't eat too cold right from the freezer — let the ice cream "dance" a bit at room temperature!

9. **Tips from Captain Marengo the Frosty:**
— Bananas are the best base for sugar-free and cream-free ice cream.
— Want a chocolate flavor? Add a spoonful of cocoa or grated chocolate.
— If the ice cream has hardened, give it 5 minutes to "thaw" before serving.

10. **Arrr! Sweet victory! Ice cream under the sails is ready!**

This is not just a dessert — it's a culinary journey through the Caribbean islands, where pirates enjoyed ice cream under the palms, watching the sunset. You've created your own sweet treasure — and it cools better than the wind from the open ocean!

Landing complete! Rum-flavored ice cream — a true tropical masterpiece!

Now you're not just a cook, but a pirate-cooler! To new desserts, adventures, and treats in the "Pirate Kitchen"!

Sorrel: a magical drink made from hibiscus and spices for true pirates!

1. **Arrr, young sailor! Today we are brewing not just any tea, but a true pirate elixir — Sorrel!**

This drink was made in the Caribbean islands during celebrations and after long voyages. It refreshes like an ocean breeze, smells of spices, and has a color as deep as the red sun over Tortuga. Sorrel is made from hibiscus flowers (also known as "Sudanese rose"), with ginger, cinnamon, nutmeg, and a touch of sweetness. Ready for the magic of the drink that pirates themselves drank?

2. **Gathering tropical ingredients — pirate provisions:**

— 1 cup of dried hibiscus flowers (sorrel)
— 3 cups of water
— 1–2 thin slices of ginger (peeled)
— 1 cinnamon stick (or 1/2 tsp ground)
— a pinch of nutmeg (ground)
— 2 tbsp honey or sugar (to taste)
— (optional) a few cloves
— lime or orange slices — for garnish

3. **Preparing to brew — a magical teapot or pot in the galley.**

Pour water into a small pot. Place it on the stove (with an adult helper!). Add ginger, a cinnamon stick, and a pinch of nutmeg. Once the water starts boiling, reduce the heat and add the hibiscus. It needs to simmer for 5–7 minutes on low heat — so the drink takes on the color of a Caribbean sunset.

4. **Watch out, captain! The magic begins — the color changes!**

While the Sorrel is brewing, the whole kitchen will be filled with a spicy aroma. The hibiscus will turn the water red, like a pirate flag! Don't forget: the pot is hot, so work only with an adult's permission. Let them remove the pot from the heat.

5. Infusion — time for the chest of aromas.

Cover the pot with a lid and let the drink infuse for another 15–20 minutes. During this time, the spices will release their essence, and the hibiscus will impart its color. You can imagine pirates sitting on the deck, waiting for their favorite tea after a storm.

6. Straining, like true Caribbean alchemists.

Ask an adult to strain the drink through a sieve or cheesecloth into a large jug. All the flowers and spices will remain in the sieve, leaving a fragrant, bright liquid in the jug. It looks like a magical ruby juice!

7. Adding sweetness — a pirate's secret in every drop!

Add honey or sugar to the warm drink to taste. Stir with a wooden spoon. Sorrel can be a bit tart — like a wild wind — so a little sweetness will make it gentle, like a lagoon at dawn.

8. Cooling — a true adventure in the hold!

Place the jug in the refrigerator for 1–2 hours. Sorrel tastes best cold, especially when it's hot outside, and the imaginary sea voyage is just beginning!

9. Serving — in glasses of pirate honor!

Pour the drink into clear glasses, add ice cubes, a slice of lime or orange on the side, a mint leaf on top — and voila! You can insert a straw or even make a paper umbrella — for a festive mood.

10. Sea advice from Grandma Hibiscus:

— Don't add too much nutmeg — just a little is needed.
— If you don't like ginger, you can add just a small piece.
— Hibiscus can be found in pharmacies or tea shops — look for "Sudanese rose" or "hibiscus."

Hooray! Sorrel is ready — your first pirate drink!

This is not just tea, but a true elixir of Caribbean mood! It was drunk by the fire on the shore, singing pirate songs and sharing stories about hidden treasures. Now you are part of this delicious legend. To new drinks and adventures, captain!

Escovitch Fish: Jamaican Fried Fish with a Spicy Marinade!

1. Yo-ho-ho, Captain! Today in the galley — the legendary Jamaican dish: Escovitch Fish!

This dish was loved by pirates in Jamaica for its crispy fish and spicy vegetable marinade. It was prepared after great victories or at shore celebrations. Escovitch is not just a dish, it's a true taste boarding: crunchy, spicy, vibrant. Put on your apron — and let's set sail on a culinary voyage!

2. Supplies from the Captain's Chest: Ingredients for the Adventure!
— 2 fillets of white fish (e.g., tilapia, dorado, hake)
— Juice of 1 lime (for marinade)
— Salt and black pepper
— Flour — for breading
— Oil for frying

For the marinade:
— 1 carrot
— 1/2 onion
— 1/2 bell pepper (yellow or red)
— 1/2 tsp mustard seeds
— A few black peppercorns
— A slice of chili (optional)
— 3-4 tbsp vinegar (apple or white)
— 1/2 cup water
— 1/2 tsp sugar
— A pinch of salt

3. **Preparing the Fish — The First Step to Victory!**

Rinse the fish, pat dry with a towel, and drizzle with lime juice. Then salt, pepper, and let it sit for 10 minutes — this is a small marination. The fish should be juicy and fresh, like a morning by the lagoon!

4. **Frying — A Hot Battle in the Galley!**

Coat the fish in flour on both sides. Ask an adult to heat a pan with oil. When it's hot, carefully place the fish. Fry for 3–4 minutes on each side until the crust is golden, like a pirate's treasure chest. Place the cooked fish on a paper towel to remove excess oil.

5. **Vegetable Boarding — Preparing the Marinade!**

Cut the carrot into strips, the onion into half-rings, and the pepper into strips. If adding chili — just a little, and only with the permission of an adult helper! In a small pot, combine vinegar, water, salt, sugar, peppercorns, and mustard seeds. Bring the mixture to a boil (with an adult), then add the vegetables and simmer for 2–3 minutes. The vegetables should remain crunchy — like sails in the wind!

6. **Combining Fish with Marinade — Like a Captain with a Ship!**

Place the fish on a plate or in a deep bowl. Evenly spread the warm vegetables with the marinade on top along with the liquid. Let it sit for 5–10 minutes — or even longer, so all the flavors meld together like pirates under the flag of brotherhood!

7. **Secrets of Caribbean Marinade — From Grandma in Port Royal!**

— Mustard seeds give an interesting aroma — don't overdo it.
— If you don't like sour, add a bit more sugar.
— Instead of lime, you can use lemon — but lime is more piquant and tropical!

8. **Safety — The Main Thing Even for a Brave Young Sailor!**

— The pan is hot! Only an adult should fry the fish.

— The vinegar and spices can have a strong aroma — don't inhale over the steam.
— Always wash your hands after working with fish and chili — pirates don't cry, but eyes sting from the heat!

9. Serving — Bright, Festive, Like a Real Pirate Feast!

Serve the fish with rice, fried plantains, sweet potatoes, or just with crispy bread. On top — vegetable marinade, on the side — a slice of lime and greens. Serve in Caribbean style — you can lay everything on a wooden board or decorate with shells!

10. Hooray, Captain! Escovitch Fish — Conquered!

This is not just a dish — it's part of Jamaican culture, where each ingredient has its taste, character, and legend. Now you know how to make crispy, aromatic, spicy fish — worthy of a pirate's table. To new taste boardings, Captain!

Escovitch Fish — Bright, Spicy, and Unforgettable!

You have prepared a dish that carries the spirit of the islands and freedom. Serve with a smile and the pride of a true pirate-chef!

Toto: Coconut Pie with the Taste of Jamaica and Pirate Adventures!

1. Yo-ho-ho, Captain! Today we're baking "Toto" — a thick Jamaican pie with coconut and spices!

This dessert was invented in Jamaica when simple but delicious ingredients were left in the hold: coconut, brown sugar, spices, and flour. Pirates baked it in iron pots right on the coals — and we will do it in the oven (and much safer!). Ready for a sweet culinary journey? Hoist the sails!

2. Supplies from the tropical island — here's what we need:

— 1.5 cups of flour
— 1 cup of grated coconut (dry or fresh)
— 1/2 cup of brown sugar
— 1 tsp of cinnamon
— 1/2 tsp of nutmeg (ground)
— 1 tsp of baking powder
— a pinch of salt
— 1 egg
— 1/2 cup of milk (can be coconut milk)
— 3 tbsp of melted butter or oil

3. Let's prepare the dough — a magical mix of tropical treasures!

In a large bowl, mix flour, coconut, sugar, cinnamon, nutmeg, baking powder, and salt. This is our "dry crew." Then, in a separate bowl, combine the egg, milk, and melted butter. This is the "wet crew." Add the wet ingredients to the dry ones and mix with a spoon. The dough will be thick — almost like pirate dough for building cookie towers!

4. The baking form — like a real hold!

Grease the baking form with oil or line it with parchment (it's like the ship's floor — nothing should stick!). Place the dough in the form and smooth it with a spoon. If you want, sprinkle a little more coconut or sugar on top for a pirate crust.

5. We send the pie into the oven ocean!

Ask an adult to turn on the oven to 180°C. Bake for about 25–30 minutes until the pie is golden on top and a knife inserted in the center comes out clean. While the dough is baking, the air is filled with the aroma of adventure, spices, and the tropics!

6. Secrets of the old coconut cook from Jamaica:

— It's better to use freshly grated coconut, but dried will also do.
— Don't overdo it with nutmeg — you need just a pinch.
— Want more tropical flavor? Add a little vanilla extract or a drop of lime juice!

7. Caution in the galley — as always, is key!

— The oven is hot as a volcano! Only an adult should take out the pie.
— Don't touch the form with your hands — even after 5 minutes, it's still burning!
— Don't taste the raw dough — real pirates wait until the end!

8. Waiting for cooling — time for pirate patience!

Let "Toto" cool a bit (15–20 minutes), then cut it into squares or triangles. You can even shape them like sails, stars, or ships — anything that reminds you of distant seas!

9. Serving — like at a pirate sweet feast!

Serve "Toto" with a mug of warm milk, herbal tea, or fruit juice. You can decorate with coconut flakes, a drop of honey, or powdered sugar (like pirate gold dust!).

10. Hooray! "Toto" is ready — and you are a true captain of baking!

You have prepared a real Jamaican dessert that holds the aroma of the sun, spices, and pirate stories. Its taste is a journey without a ship, only with a spoon in hand. Greet your crew with a sweet piece and get ready for the next culinary expedition!

"Toto" — a tropical pie that conquered the hearts and stomachs of pirates!

You have learned to make a sweet Caribbean wonder that was enjoyed under the palms five centuries ago. To new delicious boardings, Captain-Cook!

Guava Duff: a sweet roll with tropical jam that impresses even sea monsters!

1. **Hello, young pirate! Today we are making Guava Duff — a Caribbean roll with a sweet filling!**

Guava Duff is a traditional dessert from the Bahamas. It was made on ships during celebrations, especially when the captain returned from a long voyage. The filling is guava jam, and the dough is as soft as sails at dawn! Don't worry if you can't find guava — pirates always had backup tropical plans!

2. **Treasures from the tropics — here's what we need:**

— 2 cups of flour
— 1 tbsp of sugar
— 1/2 tsp of salt
— 1.5 tsp of baking powder
— 2 tbsp of butter (or oil)
— 3/4 cup of milk
— 1/2 cup of guava jam (or substitute: strawberry, apple, or pineapple)
— a bit of cinnamon for the filling (optional)
— (optional) orange or lime zest

3. **Preparing the dough — as soft as the sand on the island!**

In a large bowl, mix flour, baking powder, salt, and sugar. Add butter and rub with your hands until the dough resembles sandy lumps. Then gradually add milk and mix with a spoon, then with your hands, until the dough becomes soft and elastic. Like playdough — only tastier!

4. **Rolling out — like unfolding a treasure map!**

Sprinkle a little flour on the table and roll out the dough into a rectangle shape — about 0.5 cm thick. Now it's time for the treasure — the jam!

5. **The filling — guava sweetness (or its pirate substitute!)**

Evenly spread the guava jam over the surface of the dough. If you don't have it, use strawberry, apricot, or apple jam. Even banana-chocolate spread will do — pirates always improvise! You can sprinkle a bit of cinnamon or add zest for the aroma of distant islands.

6. **Rolling the roll — with a captain's move!**

Carefully, from one long side, roll the dough into a roll. Press lightly so the jam doesn't spill out. Pinch the edges so no one escapes from the "jam ship"!

7. **Steaming, not baking — here's where the real magic of Guava Duff is!**

This roll is unusual because it's steamed! Wrap it in greased parchment or foil, like a pirate map. Then place it in a large pot with a rack or sieve inside (so it doesn't touch the water), pour a little water at the bottom, and cover with a lid. Ask an adult to put it on the heat. Steam for about 1 hour. Check the water from time to time — don't let it evaporate!

8. **Be careful, young sailor! Hot steam is no place for carelessness!**

- Never open the lid yourself when there's steam inside. - Always work with an adult, as the pot will be hot. - Don't keep your face over the steam — even pirates protect their captain's hats from steam!

9. **Serving — like at a royal pirate feast!**

When the roll is ready, let it cool a bit, then unwrap and slice into rounds. You can drizzle a little condensed milk, sprinkle with coconut, or top with a scoop of ice cream. This will be the sweet finale of the culinary adventure!

10. **Tips from Pirate Jemka — the sweet legend of the Caribbean:**

- Don't make the dough too runny — it should hold its shape. - You can add a bit of cinnamon or cloves to the water in the steamer — the aroma will be even more tropical! - Want some color? Add a spoonful of beet juice or grated carrot to the jam — pirates loved colorful dishes!

Hooray, Guava Duff is ready!

You have just made a real Caribbean pirate dessert — soft, warm, aromatic, like a memory of a sunny island. And even if you didn't have guava, you managed to make something special with what you had on hand. To new sweet expeditions, captain-chef!

Barbary Pirates

1. **Breakfast in the Pirate Fortress: bread, olives, and spices.**

Barbary pirates from the coasts of North Africa — Algeria, Tunisia, Morocco — started their day with a traditional breakfast resembling a small feast. Freshly baked "khobz" bread or barley flatbreads were served with olive oil, honey, and salty olives. Goat cheese and dates were often added. The drink of choice was mint tea or sage infusion. For pirates at sea, dried fish or spiced jerky served as an energy snack before a stormy day.

2. **Fish Soup "Harira with Gifts of the Sea": Mediterranean Inspiration.**

For lunch, they often prepared a sea version of the famous "harira" — a soup with chickpeas, lentils, tomatoes, and a plethora of spices. If seafood was available, pieces of squid, crab, or fish were added. The broth was rich and thick, with hints of cinnamon, ginger, and saffron. Such a soup replenished the pirates' strength after sea raids and provided warmth even on windy days.

3. **Main Course: "Chermoula Fish" with Coastal Aromas.**

For dinner, coastal pirates prepared fish in a chermoula marinade — a mixture of parsley, garlic, paprika, cumin, lemon juice, and olive oil. The fish (often sardine, bass, or sea bream) was fried or baked in a clay pot. The dish was served with couscous or bread to soak up the juicy sauce. It was a feast for the stomach and the spirit — as the marinade filled the air with aromas of the distant desert and warm sea.

4. **Side Dishes: Couscous with a Sea Twist.**

Couscous — a fine wheat grain — was the main side dish for any meal. For pirates, it was prepared with vegetables, chickpeas, and pieces of fish or shellfish

Sometimes raisins or dried apricots were added to balance the spiciness. Fried eggplants and peppers with garlic were also popular — light yet hearty additions to the fish meal.

5. Snack on the Go: Fish Kebabs.

For a quick meal, Barbary pirates used fish, skewered, marinated, and grilled over an open flame. Such kebabs of anchovies or mackerel were often complemented with harissa sauce — a spicy paste of chili, garlic, and spices. They were eaten on the ship, at the market, or even during battle gatherings — food for warriors with a spirit of spices.

6. Beverages: Tea Ritual of Pirate Tribes.

Instead of alcohol, Barbary pirates valued green tea with mint. It was brewed in tall metal teapots and poured from a height to create foam. They drank from small glasses, often with added sugar or honey. It was not just a drink but a true ritual: tea symbolized respect, focus, and friendship among sea comrades.

7. Deserts from the Desert: Date Balls and Honey Treats.

After dinner, pirates enjoyed desserts that did not spoil in the hot climate. The most popular were date balls with nuts and honey. They also made "chebakia" — flower-shaped cookies soaked in rose syrup and sprinkled with sesame seeds. These sweets were not only delicious but also energetic — perfect for long journeys.

8. Shared Dinner on the Shore — A Sacred Tradition.

After returning from a voyage, pirates gathered around the fire. Someone played the flute, others cleaned fish. Everyone prepared the food together: one made the marinade, another tended the fire. It was not just dinner but a way to maintain unity, exchange news, and remember home, where similar dishes always awaited.

9. Food as Strategy: Preserving the Gifts of the Sea.

Barbary pirates were skilled at preserving food. Fish was sun-dried or smoked with spices. Sea mollusks and octopuses were marinated in vinegar with garlic. These dishes were taken to sea — they did not spoil and provided strength even during long port sieges or sea battles.

10. **Maghreb Pirates' Cuisine — A Legacy of the Mediterranean and the Desert.**

Barbary maritime cuisine is a blend of sea gifts and desert aromas. It developed at the crossroads of paths: Arab, African, Andalusian, and even Viking. Every spice, every dish tells a story of travels, battles, and friendship. Eating like a Barbary pirate means tasting the Mediterranean Sea.

The cuisine of Barbary pirates is a culinary adventure that leads us through spices, seas, and sands. It taught not to waste, to value the simple and fresh, and to share. In every piece of fish, drop of tea, or date candy, a piece of pirate wisdom is hidden. Shared food is the strongest anchor that keeps the crew together even in the stormiest waves.

Fish in a Tagine: A Barbarian Feast for the Desert Pirates!

1. **Yo-ho-ho! Preparing for a pirate journey to Morocco!**

Hello, young culinary captain! Today we are sailing not by sea, but by caravan through the sand to the barbarian cities. In this adventure, you will learn to cook fish in a tagine — a magical pot, resembling a pyramid, where the dish slowly simmers and smells like the market in Marrakech! But as always: safety is our ship, and an adult helper is our second captain. Ready for a culinary miracle? Let's begin!

2. **Ingredients — treasures from the barbarian bazaar.**

Here's the list of goodies:
— 2 fish fillets (sea bass, dorado, or hake)
— 1 carrot
— 1 potato
— 1 tomato
— 1/2 onion
— 1/2 lemon or Moroccan preserved lemon
— 2 tablespoons olive oil
— spices: cumin, coriander, paprika, a bit of turmeric
— salt, pepper
— fresh herbs (cilantro, parsley)

3. **What is a tagine and how to tame it?**

A tagine is a clay pot with a conical lid. If you don't have one, don't worry — replace it with a deep pan with a lid. But true barbarian pirates say: "In a tagine, the dish sings!" So, if you have this pot at home, you are a true Sahara chef!

4. **Marinating the fish — like the ancient barbarians.**

In a bowl, mix: 1 spoon of oil, lemon juice, a pinch of salt, paprika, turmeric, a bit of cumin. Rub this mixture onto the fish. It should rest for 15 minutes so the spices make it aromatic, as if it strolled through the streets of Fez!

5. **Preparing the vegetables — the paint for our culinary mosaic.**

Peel the carrot and potato, cut into circles (like the wheels of a pirate cannon!). Onion — into half rings. Tomato — into slices. Layer everything in the tagine: first a bit of onion, then potato, carrot, tomatoes.

6. **Building a fish pyramid.**

Place the fish on top of the vegetables. Between them — pieces of lemon or finely chopped preserved lemon. This will give the dish that Moroccan "explosion of flavor" that captivates even the stern desert pirates. Drizzle the remaining marinade and a bit of oil on top.

7. **The secret of simmering — cook slowly, like the barbarians in an oasis.**

Close the tagine with the lid. Place on the stove over low heat. Cook for 30-40 minutes, do not open often — the moisture inside cooks everything like in a magical oven! If needed, you can add a few spoons of water to the bottom.

8. **A trick from old pirate Abdul!**

Want the fish to have an even richer flavor? Add 1 olive or a pinch of coriander towards the end of cooking. Pirates say: "He who knows spices rules the kitchen!"

9. **Serving — on a carpet of aromas!**

Uncover the tagine — steam rises like a genie from a lamp! Be careful: it's hot! Serve the fish with vegetables on a plate or eat directly from the tagine (as the barbarians do), dipping bread into the sauce. Garnish with herbs — and let everyone around smell the aroma of your pirate culinary feat!

10. **Tips and safety in the desert and in the kitchen.**

— The tagine is hot! Ask an adult to remove the lid.
— Remember: spices are like gunpowder for pirates: a little is good, a lot is dangerous!
— If there is no preserved lemon — no worries. Just add more lemon juice.
— Always wash your hands before and after cooking — even pirates do it!

And now — your fish in a tagine is ready!

It smells like the spices of a Moroccan bazaar and tastes like the story of pirates who found a new home among the dunes. Bon appétit, young barbarian captain! The next culinary journey awaits you with a new recipe and a new wind!

Seafood with Couscous: A Meal of the Sea Barbary Pirates!

1. **Sail the Winds! Today — a culinary raid into coastal waters!**

Greetings, young pirate! Your mission is to prepare a dish enjoyed by the sea Barbary pirates — brave travelers who knew how to cook deliciously with the gifts of the sea and desert. We will prepare seafood with couscous! But first and foremost — safe preparation: clean hands, shiny dishes, and an adult helper at the ready. Time to set sail on a culinary voyage!

2. **Treasure in a Bag: What Do You Need?**

Here are the ingredients:
— 150 g of dry couscous
— 1 tablespoon of olive oil
— 1 small onion
— 1 clove of garlic
— 1/2 red pepper
— 1 tomato or some tomato puree
— 150 g of seafood (shrimp, squid, mussels — can be frozen)
— salt, pepper, turmeric, cumin, paprika
— juice of 1/2 lemon
— a bit of greens (parsley or cilantro)

3. **What is Couscous and Why Do Pirates Love It?**

Couscous is small balls of semolina. It is loved in the desert because it cooks quickly and easily, and with seafood, it tastes perfect! The main thing is not to over-dry it. Then it is fluffy like sea foam.

4. **Cooking Couscous — Sahara Sand on Your Plate.**

Pour couscous into a large bowl. Add a pinch of salt, 1 spoon of oil, and mix. Pour hot water (approximately 1:1), cover with a lid or plate, and leave for 5–7 minutes. Then fluff with a fork — done! Fluffy and fragrant, like golden sand.

5. **Cooking Vegetables — Bright Colors for the Dish.**

Chop the onion, garlic, pepper, and tomato finely. Ask an adult to heat a pan with a spoon of oil. First, fry the onion with garlic until golden. Add the pepper and tomato. Stew everything together for a few minutes until it becomes soft and aromatic.

6. **Time for the Sea Catch — Adding Seafood!**

Add seafood to the vegetables. If they are frozen, let them thaw a bit in advance. Fry everything for 5–7 minutes until the seafood becomes pink and juicy. Do not overcook — they cook quickly!

7. **Pirate Trick: Spices — The Heart of the Dish!**

Add a pinch of salt, a pinch of turmeric, a bit of cumin, and paprika. Mix everything — the aroma will be such that even seagulls will come to sniff. Squeeze a bit of lemon juice for freshness. Everything is delicious, like the day of capturing a spice-laden trade ship!

8. **Combining Shore and Sea — Couscous + Seafood.**

Now the most interesting part: place the couscous on a plate or in a large bowl, top with vegetables and seafood. Sprinkle with fresh greens. It looks like a pirate banquet near the Barbary fortress on the ocean shore!

9. **Secrets of the Barbary Pirate Chefs.**

— Couscous loves water: don't let it dry out.
— Seafood doesn't tolerate long cooking — cook quickly.
— Add a bit of chili if you want to make the dish "fiery," like a real boarding!
— If there is no seafood, you can use chicken or vegetables.

10. **Safety in the Kitchen — As Important as on a Ship!**

— The pan is hot, so entrust it to an adult helper.
— A sharp knife is not for little pirates. Cut only under supervision.
— Sprinkle spices moderately — a pirate's heart should be brave, but not burn the tongue!
— Always wash your hands before and after work.

Hooray, Captain! Your dish is ready!

Seafood with couscous is a culinary combination of desert sand and ocean waves. It was cooked by the fires of the sea Barbary pirates, who guarded the shores and welcomed ships with the scents of mint and cinnamon. And now you are part of this delicious legend. Bon appétit, and until the next culinary journey!

Tuna with Olives and Lemon: A Treasure from the Kitchen of Barbary Pirates!

1. **Course to the North! Preparing for Adventures in the Barbary Bay!**

Greetings, young pirate! Today we will anchor near North Africa, where the Barbary pirates knew not only how to battle the desert winds but also how to prepare delicious tuna. The dish is simple yet aromatic, like a storm on the citrus coast. Remember — you are the captain of the kitchen, but stay safe: have an adult helmsman nearby to assist with hot and sharp tasks!

2. **A Treasure for the Recipe — Preparing the Ingredients.**

Find these products in your kitchen:
— 2 pieces of fresh or canned tuna (not in oil!)
— 1/2 lemon
— 6–8 pitted olives (green or black)
— 1 small onion
— 1 clove of garlic
— 1 tablespoon of olive oil
— spices: turmeric, paprika, cumin, salt, pepper
— herbs: parsley or cilantro

3. **Tuna — the Traveling Fish!**

Tuna is a true sea traveler, just like pirates. It is fast, strong, and tasty! Today we will prepare it in the Barbary style: simple, aromatic, with a hint of sun and spices.

4. **Preparing the Marinade — The Magic of Spices!**

In a small bowl, mix: the juice of half a lemon, a pinch of turmeric, a bit of paprika, a pinch of cumin, a pinch of salt, and a tablespoon of oil. Add minced garlic. Be careful: garlic can "bite" your eyes if you rub them after cutting! Rub the tuna with this mixture. Let it sit for 10–15 minutes to absorb the aroma of adventure.

5. Time for Chopping — Work Like a Careful Helmsman.

Slice the onion into half-rings and the olives into circles. Ask an adult to help with the sharp knife. This will be your dish-schooner: the onion as sails, and the olives as black cannons!

6. Frying the Tuna — It Sizzles Like a Pirate Cannon!

Ask an adult to place the pan on medium heat and add a bit of oil. When the oil is hot, place the tuna. Fry for 2–3 minutes on each side if it's fresh tuna. If canned, just heat it together with the onion and olives in the pan.

7. Gathering the Whole Crew of Flavor!

Add the onion and olive slices to the tuna. Mix everything carefully so the pieces don't fall apart. Drizzle a bit of leftover lemon juice on top — and the dish will sing with the aroma of the Mediterranean Sea!

8. Serving — A Tablecloth Instead of a Treasure Map!

Place the tuna on a plate, garnish with herbs and a few lemon slices. It can be served with bulgur, couscous, or just warm bread. And if you have a fresh cucumber on hand — it will be the perfect companion for the tuna!

9. Secrets of the Barbary Pirate Chefs.

— Do not overcook the tuna — it will become dry like an old sail.
— Always add lemon at the end — the taste will be fresh, not bitter.
— Olives can be replaced with capers if you want more "pirate tanginess."
— Parsley or cilantro is added at the end — so the aroma doesn't disappear!

10. Safety Tips for the Pirate-Chef.

— A sharp knife and hot pan — only with an adult on board!
— Do not leave the stove unattended, even if you're curious about what's in the fridge.
— After cutting garlic and lemon — always wash your hands!
— Sprinkle spices carefully — pirates have a sense of smell and taste too, don't turn the fish into a volcano!

Tuna with Olives and Lemon — the Dish of a True Barbary Captain!

It is fresh, juicy, and smells of the sea, lemons, and adventures. When you taste it — it's like sitting by a campfire under the stars of the Sahara, with old pirates telling their stories nearby. Bon appétit, brave chef! Prepare the helm for new culinary journeys!

Crab Balls with Hummus: A Crunchy Treasure of the Barbary Shores!

1. Ahoy, sailor! We're cooking a dish from the treasures of the sea and desert!

Greetings, young pirate! Today we will anchor in the land of spices and hot sun — on the Barbary coasts. There, pirates knew how to combine the gifts of the sea with the secrets of desert cuisine. We will prepare **crab balls with hummus** — a dish that combines the crunchy sea and the gentle power of chickpeas! But first — call an adult helper to ensure the kitchen adventure is safe. Prepare for a taste boarding!

2. Pirate's list of ingredients.

Here's what to find in the holds:
— 200 g of crab meat or crab sticks
— 1 egg
— 1/2 cup of breadcrumbs (and a bit more for coating)
— 1 small onion or green onion
— 1 clove of garlic
— 1 tablespoon of mayonnaise or Greek yogurt
— salt, pepper, paprika
— oil for frying

For hummus:
— 1 can of cooked chickpeas
— 1 tablespoon of olive oil
— 1 tablespoon of lemon juice
— 1 clove of garlic
— a pinch of salt, turmeric, cumin

3. Crab balls — like cannonballs, but tasty!

Chop the crab meat or sticks very finely — like an old pirate grinding his musket ball. Mince the onion, add to the crab. Beat the egg, add mayonnaise or yogurt, a clove of garlic (pressed or finely chopped), and spices: a bit of salt, pepper, paprika. Then add breadcrumbs until the mixture resembles plasticine. If it's too soft — add a bit more breadcrumbs.

4. Forming the balls — roll them like a pirate's pearl!

With wet hands (so nothing sticks), roll small balls — slightly larger than a coin. Coat them in breadcrumbs. They look like real sea treasures!

5. Frying — beware, they sizzle like a sea wave!

Pour a bit of oil (2–3 tablespoons) into a pan and heat it. Ask an adult to help. Fry the balls on all sides until golden brown — about 2 minutes on each side. Transfer to a paper towel to remove excess fat. Smell that? It's success!

6. And now — hummus: a cream of chickpeas and spices.

In a blender, mix cooked chickpeas, a tablespoon of oil, lemon juice, garlic, a pinch of salt, turmeric, and a pinch of cumin. Blend everything into a creamy mass. If it's too thick — add a bit of water. The hummus should be as gentle as the sand under your feet on a warm Barbary beach.

7. Serving secrets from Barbary chefs.

Place a bit of hummus on a plate, make a "floating island" of crab balls in the center. Drizzle with olive oil, garnish with a parsley leaf or pomegranate seeds — if available. This will be a true culinary fleet on a lemon sea!

8. Pirate tricks and culinary tips.

— It's better to blend hummus slowly, then it will be tender.
— If there's no blender — ask an adult to mash the chickpeas with a fork, it will be "home style".
— You can add a bit of grated cheese to the crab balls — it will be even tastier!
— If you don't like mayonnaise — replace it with a spoonful of mashed potatoes.

9. Safety watch — captain, be vigilant!

— Frying is a serious matter. Never approach hot oil without an adult.
— Always wash your hands after working with eggs and raw products.
— Sharp objects — only under the control of an experienced adult pirate!

10. When the dish is ready — a celebration on the ship!

Taste: tender crab balls and hummus with a spicy flavor — like a journey on a Barbary ship along the African coast. The flavors combine like a compass and stars. Eat slowly, enjoy every bite — and remember this recipe as your pirate culinary map!

Crab balls with hummus — a delicious stop on the Barbary shores!

This is not just a dish — it's a sea adventure with notes of spices, hot sand, and winds from distant deserts. Bon appétit, young chef! Many more gastronomic islands lie ahead!

Squid and Mint Soup: A Refreshing Dish of the Barbary Pirates!

1. Ahoy, young captain! Today we're cooking a soup known only to the pirates of the northern shores!

We dive into the waves of the Mediterranean Sea, where Barbary pirates loved to combine the gifts of the sea with fresh herbs. Our recipe is **squid and mint soup**. It's light, aromatic, and refreshing even on a hot day in the desert. Remember the main rule of pirate cuisine: **safety first!** Sharp objects and hot stoves — only with an adult helper on board!

2. What you'll need — treasures from the pirate's pantry:

Find these ingredients:
— 200 g of squid (cleaned, fresh or frozen)
— 1 medium potato
— 1 carrot
— 1 small onion
— 1 clove of garlic
— 1 tablespoon of olive oil
— 4-5 fresh mint leaves
— spices: salt, pepper, a pinch of turmeric or paprika
— water (approximately 800 ml)

3. Getting to know the squid — pirates respect them!

Squids are intelligent and fast creatures of the sea. If you're using frozen ones, ask an adult to defrost them in cold water. Then they need to be cut into rings — carefully, like carving a pirate ring from a shell!

4. Preparing the vegetables — setting up the shore base.

Peel the potato, carrot, and onion. Cut into small cubes or slices. Ask an adult to help with the knife. This will be the base of our soup, like the deck is the base of a ship.

5. Magical sautéing — aroma throughout the galley!

Heat a tablespoon of oil in a pot. Ask an adult to help. First, sauté a bit of onion and garlic until golden. Then add the carrot and potato. Stir and cook for a few minutes until the vegetables are soft. Add a pinch of turmeric — it will give a golden color, like treasure in the sand!

6. Pouring in the water — a wave of flavor!

Add approximately 800 ml of water to the vegetables. Let it boil. Then reduce the heat and simmer the soup for 10 minutes until the vegetables are soft. It's time to tune into the sea wave of aroma!

7. Time for the squid — from the depths of the ocean to your plate!

Add the sliced squid to the soup. They should be cooked for no more than 2-3 minutes — otherwise, they'll become tough. Squids are ready when they are white and tender. Watch carefully not to overcook!

8. Mint — a pirate's dawn in a bowl!

Tear a few mint leaves with your hands (this preserves the aroma better) and add to the soup at the very end. You can add a bit more fresh greens on top. Mint will add lightness, as if you're sailing on a sailboat in the dawn sea!

9. Serving — pouring into bowls like a true captain!

Turn off the stove (again — an adult on guard!). Pour the soup into a deep bowl, add a mint leaf or a pinch of paprika on top. If you have a piece of bread or flatbread — dip it into the broth. The flavors melt like mist over the sea!

10. Tips and pirate warnings:

— Don't cook the squid for long — they're quick like a sea whirl.
— Don't throw mint into boiling water, as it will lose its aroma. Add it at the very end.
— Sharp knife, hot pot — only with an adult helper!
— Always wash your hands after working with seafood. And don't forget: wash your hands before eating — even pirates don't want to get sick!

Squid and mint soup — a light sip of the sea for a true Barbary pirate!

This dish refreshes, warms, and gives a sense of adventure. It's as unusual as a seagull over a ship and as pleasant as the coolness under a sail on a hot day. You are now not just a cook, but a sea herbalist! To new adventures, captain!

Baked Sardines with Cumin: A Pirate Dish from the Barbary Wharf!

1. We dock at the fish market! The sardine adventure begins!

Hello, young pirate! Today we will set sail to the shores where Barbary fishermen caught sardines and prepared them simply but deliciously — **with cumin, lemon, and fire!** This is a dish you can eat with your hands, like a true sailor. But remember: you need to handle fish and fire carefully, so call an adult helper to the galley!

2. The treasure map of ingredients:

What you need to find in your provisions:
— 6-8 fresh sardines (or frozen, already cleaned)
— 1 teaspoon of cumin
— 1 teaspoon of paprika
— 1 clove of garlic
— juice of half a lemon
— 1-2 tablespoons of olive oil
— a pinch of salt
— fresh herbs for serving (parsley or cilantro)

3. Getting to know sardines — small fish, big taste!

Sardines are small sea fish that are very rich in benefits. If they are not cleaned — ask an adult to help. Cleaning a sardine is like opening a shell with a pearl: remove the head and guts, rinse, and the fish is ready for spices!

4. Preparing the pirate marinade — a magical sauce for sailors!

In a bowl, mix: minced garlic, cumin, paprika, salt, lemon juice, and olive oil. This will be our seasoning — as spicy as an old pirate's tale by the fire! Mix everything thoroughly with a spoon. You are the master of spices!

5. Rubbing the sardines — not with a sword, but with marinade!

Place the fish on a plate and rub it with the marinade on both sides. If the sardines are small, they can be baked whole. Leave for 10 minutes so the spices can "whisper" their secrets to the fish.

6. **Preparation for baking — an oven instead of a ship's cannon!**

Turn on the oven to 180°C (an adult can do this). Place the sardines on a baking sheet lined with parchment paper or greased with oil. If you want, you can cover them with foil — this will make them more tender. Bake for 15–20 minutes until the fish turns golden.

7. **Serving — like at a Barbary feast!**

When the sardines are ready, place them on a plate. Garnish with finely chopped herbs and lemon rings. You can serve with bread or couscous. In Barbary families, such fish is eaten with hands — pirate style!

8. **Secrets of the kitchen from coastal towns.**

— Cumin is the main hero. It gives the fish a warm, "earthy" aroma.
— Use sweet paprika, not hot — so as not to "burn the ship."
— Sardines cook quickly, so make sure they don't dry out.
— If you want an adventure — add a little dried thyme or rosemary.

9. **Tips for the young pirate-chef:**

— The marinade can be a little tangy — try it with your finger (just don't forget to wash your hands!).
— Don't keep the fish in the oven longer than necessary — it's small and dries out quickly.
— If you don't like bones — ask an adult to remove them after baking.
— Always wash your hands after working with fish and garlic — even pirates love clean fingers!

10. **Safety in the galley!**

— Sharp knives and the oven are for the captain's assistant.
— Don't touch hot dishes right away — let them "cool down after the battle."
— Wash your hands and all tools thoroughly after contact with raw fish.
— Don't sniff cumin directly from the jar — it might get into your nose, and then you'll sneeze like a pirate after a storm!

Baked sardines with cumin — a humble fish with the proud heart of the sea!

This dish is like an ancient Barbary song: simple, aromatic, and warmed by the coastal sun. It tells of fishing boats returning with their catch to the bay, where bread, spices, and laughter awaited them. Now you are part of this story. Enjoy, captain! To new pirate flavors!

Sea Skewers: Pirate Fire of the Barbary Shores!

1. **To the fire, captain! Today we are cooking skewers from the depths of the sea!**

Greetings, young pirate! Today we will set sail to the Barbary coast — a place where in ancient times, boardings thundered and the delicious aroma of sea skewers filled the air! This dish is a true pirate's treat: we thread squid, shrimp, and vegetables onto a skewer, generously sprinkle with spices, and then — to the fire! But the main thing is a *safe deck*: cook only with an adult helper!

2. **What's in the sea cargo? Here are the ingredients:**

Find:
— 100 g of shrimp (peeled)
— 100 g of squid (sliced into rings)
— 1 bell pepper
— 1 small zucchini or squash
— 1/2 onion
— 2–3 tablespoons of olive oil
— juice of half a lemon
— spices: salt, pepper, cumin, paprika
— wooden skewers or metal skewers

3. **Preparing the skewer fleet — slicing the ingredients!**

Cut the pepper and zucchini into circles or squares (so that they can be easily threaded onto a skewer). Slice the onion into half-rings. It's best to defrost the seafood in advance. Everything should be as clean as a deck before a parade!

4. **Marinade — a spicy gust of wind from Barbary!**

In a deep bowl, mix: olive oil, lemon juice, a pinch of cumin, paprika, salt, and pepper. Add the seafood and vegetables, and gently mix. Leave for 10–15 minutes — let each piece absorb the aroma of the journey!

5. **Threading like pearls on a pirate necklace!**

Alternately thread onto the skewer: shrimp, squid ring, a piece of pepper, a slice of zucchini, a piece of onion. Repeat until the skewer is full. This is not just food — it's an edible fleet!

6. **Time to bake! We bake like real Barbary pirates!**

Skewers can be cooked:
— In the oven (at 200°C, 10–12 minutes)
— On a grill pan
— Or on a real barbecue if you're outdoors (then definitely with an adult captain!)

Fry on all sides until golden, but not for long — seafood is as quick as seagulls over the waves.

7. **Pirate decoration — lemon and greens!**

Place the ready skewers on a plate. You can sprinkle with lemon juice, sprinkle with greens, add sauce (for example, yogurt with mint or garlic). Presentation — like a royal boarding!

8. **Secrets of Barbary chefs:**

— Shrimp cook quickly — 2–3 minutes, no more!
— If you want tenderness — marinate longer (20 minutes).
— Soak wooden skewers in water for 10 minutes before baking to prevent burning.
— You can thread everything in any order — make your own pirate flag of taste!

9. **Caution — your main sails!**

— Hot oven and grill — a task for an adult!
— Don't touch the ready skewers immediately — they are hot!
— Work in the kitchen only on a clean surface, and always wash your hands after handling fish and shrimp.
— Don't play with raw seafood — it's not a toy, but an ingredient!

10. **Time to taste — the pirate feast is open!**

Eat the skewers straight from the skewer (carefully!), or carefully remove with a fork. With bread, sauce, or vegetables — this is real pirate food, returning after a raid with holds full of spices and seafood. Does it taste good? It's your victory in the culinary sea battle!

Sea skewers — a delicious journey along the Barbary coast!

This dish smells of the sea, wind, and adventure. It's simple but tasty — like the stories of old pirates by the fire. And remember: when you cook yourself, you're not just a cook, you're the captain of a culinary ship. To new adventures, young grill master!

Mint Mussel Salad: A Refreshing Treasure of Barbary Pirates!

1. **Ahoy, Captain! Today we will open a pirate salad port!**

On our culinary ship, the course is set for the Barbary coast, where pirates, returning from raids, feasted on a refreshing *mussel salad with mint*. This dish is light, aromatic, and very healthy! We will cook together, so call an adult helper — they will be your navigator among lemons and shells!

2. **Ingredients from the pirate market:**

Prepare:
— 200 g of cooked mussels without shells (can be frozen, thawed in advance)
— 1 fresh cucumber
— 1/2 red bell pepper
— 2–3 sprigs of fresh mint
— juice of half a lemon
— 1 tablespoon of olive oil
— a pinch of salt and pepper
— (optional) a bit of parsley or green onion

3. **Mussels — a true sea delicacy!**

These shells contain a lot of protein, iron, and iodine — everything a little pirate needs to be as strong as a schooner in a storm! If you are using ready-cooked mussels — great. If raw — ask an adult to boil them in water for 5–7 minutes until the shells open.

4. **Preparing the vegetable deck!**

Slice the cucumber into rounds or half-moons, and the pepper into cubes. Everything should be colorful, like a real pirate flag at a festival! If you want more color — add a tomato or a boiled egg. But first — a simple classic recipe.

5. **Mint — the soul of the salad and the fresh breath of the Mediterranean Sea.**

Pluck the mint leaves and tear them with your hands — not a knife! This way, the mint smells better and retains its fragrant character. Add it to the vegetables. You can add a bit of parsley for color, but mint is the main star of this dish.

6. **Gathering the treasure: mixing all the ingredients.**

In a large bowl, gently mix the cucumber, pepper, mint, and cooled mussels. Pour everything with lemon juice and olive oil. Add a pinch of salt and pepper. Now, with a spoon — gently, like a paddle in a bay — mix the salad.

7. **Pirate trick: how to make the salad even better!**

— Add a few drops of orange juice — it will be sweet and fresh.
— You can throw in pomegranate seeds — these are "ruby treasures" in the salad.
— If there is no fresh mint — a little dried will do, but don't overdo it!

8. **Serving — like at a pirate feast in Algiers!**

Place the salad on a plate, garnish with a mint leaf on top, and you can sprinkle with lemon zest. Serve with bread, pita, or in small boats made of lettuce leaves. Pirates ate quickly but with appetite!

9. **Tips from Berber pirate chefs:**

— The salad should be cool — do not leave it in the sun or near the stove.
— Lemon is added before serving so that the mint does not wilt.
— Do not mix the salad too much — it should be light and fluffy, like sea foam!

10. **Culinary safety on board!**

— Cook mussels only with an adult — raw seafood requires caution!
— Lemon juice can get into your eyes — so be careful when squeezing.
— Do not use mint if it is already wilted or yellowed — such herbs are not for a pirate meal!

Mint Mussel Salad — a refreshing treasure from the Barbary shores!

This is not just a dish — it's a light breeze on the ship's bow, a breath of wind among spices and sea foam. Such a salad was enjoyed by pirates in the heat when they needed to refresh and gather before a new raid. Bon appétit, Captain! Prepare the next culinary course — new treasures await!

Orange Dessert with Dates: A Sweet Respite for Barbary Pirates!

1. **Ahoy, Captain! It's dessert time — a sweet stop after sea battles!**

Today we stop in a Barbary city amidst orange groves and date palms. After fried fish and sea kebabs, pirates also loved something sweet. We will prepare an *orange dessert with dates* — juicy, aromatic, and simple. But even a dessert requires attention and the help of an adult assistant. Let's dive into the culinary fairy tale of the desert!

2. **What do we need? Assembling the sweet treasure:**

Search in the hold:
— 2 ripe oranges
— 6-8 soft pitted dates
— 1 teaspoon of honey (or maple syrup)
— a pinch of cinnamon
— a few mint leaves (for aroma and decoration)
— (optional) a bit of grated almonds or chopped nuts

3. **Oranges — the sun on a plate!**

Oranges need to be peeled. Ask an adult to help, as the skin can be quite thick. Then slice the oranges into rounds or wedges. Don't forget: the juice might squirt — so don't bring your hands to your eyes!

4. **Dates — sweet treasures of the desert.**

Dates need to be cut into halves or quarters. If they still have pits — let an adult remove them. Soft dates are easy to cut but tend to stick to the knife — moisten it with a bit of water!

5. **Assembling the dessert, like a treasure on a map.**

In a beautiful plate, arrange the oranges in a circle — like the sun. Place the dates in the center. Sprinkle with a pinch of cinnamon — it will smell like a market in Marrakech! If you wish, add a bit of grated nuts on top — these will be the "gold coins" of your dessert.

6. Honey drizzle — the dessert gets its magic.

Drizzle with a spoonful of honey or syrup. You can do this with a small spoon, drawing a "pattern" over the fruits — like a pirate drawing a treasure map. The honey will make everything shiny and delicious.

7. Mint — the cool breath of a Berber night.

Tear a few mint leaves (with your hands — it smells better this way!) and sprinkle on top. If you like, place a whole leaf in the center as a flag. The salad is ready to serve!

8. Serving — like in a sheikh's tent!

You can serve the dessert on a plate or in small transparent bowls. If you chill it in the fridge for 10–15 minutes — it will be even fresher! Barbary pirates loved to savor it under the stars by the campfire after a long day of travel.

9. Taste secrets — from the sweet boatswain:

— If the oranges are very sour, add a bit more honey.
— Dates can be replaced with figs or raisins.
— The aroma of cinnamon will make the dessert cozy, even in sand and wind.
— Nuts are optional but add crunch, like a pirate surprise.

10. Safety in the sweet kitchen:

— Knives — only with an adult. Even fruits are cut carefully!
— Don't overeat honey — even pirates know that too much sweet is harmful!
— Always wash fruits before cooking — even in the desert there's dust!
— After dessert — don't forget to thank your crew (adult captain)!

Orange dessert with dates — a sweet page of Barbary history!

This simple dish is a piece of the sun, sand from the desert, and wind from the citrus grove. It teaches that a dessert doesn't have to be complicated to be magical. Eat slowly, savor attentively — and continue your journey to delicious lands!

Fish Soup "Harira from the Gifts of the Sea": A Pirate Bowl of Adventures from the Barbary Coast!

1. Prepare your spoon and compass — today we are cooking pirate harira from the sea!

Greetings, young pirate! In Barbary, soups were not just dishes — they were real cauldrons of strength! Today we will prepare *fish harira with gifts of the sea* — a hot, fragrant soup that will warm you even after the wildest boarding. But remember: the stove is not a ship's toy. Be sure to invite an adult helmsman to help!

2. Preparing supplies for the culinary raid:

You will need:
— 150 g of white fish fillet (such as hake, cod, or dorado)
— 100 g of shrimp (or other seafood — mussels, squid)
— 1 carrot
— 1 small potato
— 1 tomato or a spoonful of tomato paste
— 1 small onion
— 1 clove of garlic
— 1 tablespoon of olive oil
— Spices: salt, pepper, cumin, turmeric, a bit of paprika
— Fresh parsley or cilantro
— 700–800 ml of water

3. We start with preparing the vegetables — no pirate can survive without them!

Peel the potatoes, carrots, and onions. Slice the carrots into circles, the potatoes into cubes, and chop the onion finely. The tomato can be grated or simply use tomato paste. Ask an adult to help with the knife — pirates cut only under the captain's supervision!

4. Sautéing — open fire in the cauldron!

In a deep pot (or cauldron!), heat a spoonful of oil.

Carefully add the onion and garlic, sauté until translucent. Then add the carrots, a bit of turmeric, paprika, and cumin — and everything will play with aroma, as if you are at a Berber spice market!

5. **Add water — a wave of flavor rises!**

Add the potatoes and tomatoes (or paste) to the pot, pour in the water. Salt, pepper, and let it simmer over medium heat for 10 minutes. This is the base of our harira — just a little more, and it will be like a celebration after a successful sea voyage!

6. **Sea gifts — like gold from the hold!**

Cut the fish into cubes, and carefully rinse the shrimp. When the vegetables become soft, add the fish and seafood. Cook for another 5–7 minutes — no more! Fish is quick, like a seagull in a storm — don't overcook!

7. **Greens and spices — a pirate's signature on the dish!**

Add finely chopped parsley or cilantro. Stir, taste the broth — if needed, add more spices. Turmeric gives a golden color, and cumin — the taste of travel. Berber chefs never forgot about greens — they are like a flag on the mast!

8. **Serving — a bowl with history.**

Pour the harira into a deep plate, garnish with greens on top, and place a piece of bread or flatbread on the side. For pirates, bread replaced the spoon — you can dip it right into the soup! Don't rush — let it cool a bit before the first sip!

9. **Secrets of Berber flavor:**

— If you want a thicker soup — mash some potatoes with a wooden spoon right in the pot.
— Shrimp can be replaced with fish balls or even canned tuna (add at the very end!).
— If adding squid — throw them in at the end, as they become rubbery if cooked for too long.

10. **Safety first, even in a pirate kitchen!**

— The stove is hot — an adult should control the fire!
— Prepare fish only on a clean board, and wash your hands after each stage.
— Do not touch knives and boiling water without the helmsman's permission.
— Measure spices with a spoon, not from the jar — pirates love order in their chests!

Fish harira — a warm soup that tells stories of waves and spices!

It warms, fills with strength, and leaves a taste of adventure. This soup is like a deep breathing ocean: simple on the outside, but rich inside. Bon appétit, brave cook! Many more taste raids lie ahead!

Chebakia: Sweet Flowers of the Barbary Pirates' Roses!

1. **Ahoy, sweet captain! It's time to bake flowers for the pirate feast!**

Today, our ship docked near the palaces of Barbary, where even the toughest pirates couldn't resist sweets. We will be making *chebakia* — whimsical flower-shaped cookies that, after frying, are bathed in rose syrup and covered with a rain of sesame seeds! It's a true treasure of sweet magic. But be careful: this dish requires the help of an experienced adult pirate!

2. **Supplies from the sweet hold — what you need:**

For the dough:
— 2 cups of flour
— 1/2 teaspoon of cinnamon
— 1/2 teaspoon of turmeric
— a pinch of salt
— 1 teaspoon of anise seeds (or ground)
— 2 tablespoons of sesame seeds (toasted)
— 2 tablespoons of olive or vegetable oil
— 2 tablespoons of orange juice (or a bit of flower water)
— 1/4 cup of water (approximately)
— a bit of yeast (optional — for softer dough)

For frying and decoration:
— vegetable oil (for frying)
— 1 cup of honey
— 1-2 tablespoons of rose water
— toasted sesame seeds for sprinkling

3. Dough — the magical base of the sweet flower garden.

In a large bowl, mix flour, salt, spices, anise seeds, and sesame seeds. Add oil and orange juice. Stir with a spoon, then with your hands. Gradually add water until the dough becomes soft, like sand between your fingers after rain. Knead well (with the help of an adult) — the dough should be elastic. Cover with a towel and let it "rest" for 15 minutes — like a ship in a quiet bay.

4. Forming the flowers — the most exciting part!

Roll out the dough thinly, like a pirate map. Cut into rectangles the size of a palm. Make 4–5 parallel cuts in each (not to the edge!), like a comb. Then fold the "ribbon" accordion-style, pinch the edges — and a rose or fan shape will form. It's a bit like magic — but you're the captain!

5. Frying — golden flowers in the cauldron!

In a deep pan, heat the oil (adult assistance is essential here!). Carefully place the flowers a few at a time — don't overload the boat! Fry until golden on both sides. Then remove with tongs and place on a napkin to drain the oil.

6. Honey storm with a scent of roses!

In a small pot, heat the honey (do not boil!) with rose water. Dip the hot chebakia in there for a few seconds — let them be fully covered in syrup. It's a magical bath that makes the flowers even sweeter!

7. Sesame rain — the culmination of the culinary legend!

Place the sweet flowers on a plate. Generously sprinkle with toasted sesame seeds. Everything is ready! It looks like gold and pearls from the pirate holds that sailed into the sweet kingdom!

8. Secrets from the sweet boatswain:

— To prevent chebakia from opening during frying, pinch the dough well.
— If the dough sticks, sprinkle your hands with flour.
— You can make small or large flowers — as your imagination desires!

9. Caution on the sweet boarding!

— Hot oil and honey are dangerous! Fry and dip only with an adult helper.
— Never leave the pan unattended.
— After working with flour and oil — be sure to wash your hands!
— If something doesn't work out — don't be upset, even pirates didn't discover treasures on the first try!

10. Serving — like at a palace feast under the stars of the Sahara!

Arrange the chebakia on a beautiful plate, garnish with mint leaves or a pinch of cinnamon. Serve with mint tea — just like the Barbary pirates did after a victory. One bite — and you're in a fairy tale!

Chebakia — a sweet story in the form of a flower that blooms in every bite!

This cookie is not just a treat, but a part of ancient culture, where spices, honey, and mint lived in harmony, and each flower is like a story. You're not just a cook, you're the creator of a sweet ship of dreams! To new delicious journeys, captain!

Dessert from Goat/Camel Milk: Barbarian Treasure in a Cup!

1. Ahoy, Captain! Today we're making a dessert that warmed pirates even at night in the desert!

When the Barbary pirates returned from their journeys across the sands, they enjoyed a simple yet valuable dish — *sweet dessert from goat or camel milk*. Such milk was a true treasure: nutritious, beneficial, and refreshing in the heat. Are you ready to create your little pirate culinary oasis? Then let's set sail! (And don't forget to call an adult — they're your navigator in the kitchen!)

2. What you'll need — desert ingredients:
— 2 cups of goat or camel milk (can be bought in a store or at the market)
— 1 tablespoon of cornstarch
— 1-2 teaspoons of honey or sugar
— A pinch of cardamom or cinnamon (optional)
— Chopped dates, nuts, or sesame seeds — for decoration
— A few mint leaves (for beauty and freshness)

3. Desert milk — a unique gift of nature!

Goat milk is very nutritious, easy on the stomach, and has a delicate taste. Camel milk is even more valuable, sweetish, and rare, like a treasure. Choose what you can find and get ready to brew the true magic of the desert!

4. Mixing the ingredients — the magical elixir of the Berbers.

In a small bowl, mix the cornstarch with a few tablespoons of cold milk to avoid lumps. This is our little secret for thickness. Pour the rest of the milk into a saucepan and put it on the heat along with the sugar or honey. (An adult should stand nearby — it's the hot sea of the kitchen!)

5. **Adding spices — the pirate aroma of the desert.**

When the milk becomes warm (not boiling!), add cardamom or cinnamon. Stir. Then slowly pour in the cornstarch mixture, stirring constantly. It's like raising the sails — slowly and carefully!

6. **Brewing — like cooking a potion for a journey!**

Let everything cook for another 2–3 minutes on low heat until the mixture becomes thicker, like a creamy wave. The main thing is to stir constantly so it doesn't burn! When the consistency is like liquid pudding — turn it off!

7. **Pouring into cups — like real sheikhs after a journey.**

Carefully pour the mixture into small bowls, cups, or clay pots (if you have them). Let it cool at room temperature, then put it in the fridge for 30 minutes to set. This dessert is delicious both warm and cold!

8. **Pirate decoration — small details of a big dish.**

Sprinkle finely chopped dates, almonds, or sesame seeds on top. Place a mint leaf on top — it refreshes like the wind among the dunes. If you want, drizzle a few drops of orange juice for a citrus note!

9. **Secrets and tips from nomadic chefs:**

— Don't let the milk boil — it will lose its delicate taste.
— Always dissolve the cornstarch in cold milk!
— Camel milk takes longer to cook, so stir constantly.
— If there's no cardamom — cinnamon is enough, or you can do without spices for a milder taste.

10. **Safety on the culinary ship:**

— The pot is hot — don't touch it without an adult's help.
— Don't leave the stove unattended — even in the desert, there are cautious chefs!
— Don't add honey to hot milk — better in warm or already in the bowl.
— And most importantly: always wash your hands before and after cooking — even if you're a pirate!

Barbarian milk dessert — a sweet sip of desert legend!

This is not just a dish — it's a piece of ancient history when travelers, pirates, and nomads shared a bowl of milk by the fire. It warms, refreshes, and gives a sense of peace after adventures. Enjoy, Captain! To new sweet horizons!

Somali Pirates

1. Breakfast by the Red Sea: shuro and fish at dawn.

Somali pirates started their day with a breakfast that combined energy with simplicity. A popular morning dish was "shuro" — a thick soup made from chickpea flour, oil, spices, and onions, sometimes with the addition of smoked fish. It was served with "canjeero" — a thin, pancake-like bread. Fresh fried sardines or dried fish were added for protein. The drink was sweet black tea with ginger or cardamom, without which no Somali day begins.

2. Fish and curry soup: spices with a sea aroma.

For lunch, pirates prepared a fish-based soup with the addition of curry — an aromatic spice mix. The broth included tomatoes, garlic, pepper, and sometimes coconut milk. It was made with tuna or barracuda caught off the coast. The soup was thick, served with lemon and pieces of lahoh — Somali bread with small holes that absorbed the aromatic juices. This dish was an excellent source of energy for long hours at sea.

3. Main course: fish on "basbas" rice — spicy and nutritious.

For dinner, Somali pirates often ate a dish of rice and fried fish called "basbas" — rice with spices and a sauce based on tomatoes and hot peppers. The fish, usually barracuda or mahi-mahi, was pre-marinated in garlic, lemon juice, and cumin. After frying, it was served on aromatic rice with fried onions and raisins — an unusual but beloved combination of sweet and spicy.

4. Side dishes: "maalwa" ring bread and stewed vegetables.

With fish dishes, they served "maalwa" — fried dough cakes, slightly sweet. They were convenient for eating on the go or in a boat. Pirates also often stewed carrots, potatoes, and eggplants with onions, tomatoes, and spices. These vegetables were easily accessible in coastal villages and added color and nutrition to sea dishes.

5. Sea snack: dried shark or sun-dried squid.

When fresh fish was in abundance, pirates dried it in the sun or cured it with spices. Dried shark, cut into strips and rubbed with salt and pepper, was considered special. It was chewed as a snack — a lasting taste and lots of protein. Sun-dried squid with lemon zest was also popular — a hearty dish that could be stored for a long time.

6. Beverages: cardamom tea and chilled tamarind juice.

Among the favorite drinks of Somalis was hot "shaai" tea with cardamom, ginger, and lots of sugar. They drank it in the morning, after lunch, and in the evening. In the heat, tamarind juice was refreshing: sweet and sour, refreshing, and good for the stomach. Sometimes they made infusions of mint or lemongrass — drinks that helped keep a clear mind even under the scorching sun.

7. Desserts: spiced halva and date sweets.

After dinner, pirates loved to enjoy spiced halva — a jelly-like dessert made from flour, butter, cinnamon, and cardamom. Nuts or coconut were often added. Another sweet favorite was date balls with sesame seeds. These desserts were made in coastal settlements and taken to sea because they did not spoil and provided energy.

8. Communal dinner on the beach — a tradition of brotherhood.

After a hard day, pirates gathered around a fire on the beach. They ate together, sitting around a large tray from which they took rice, fish, and vegetables — with their hands, as is customary in Somali culture

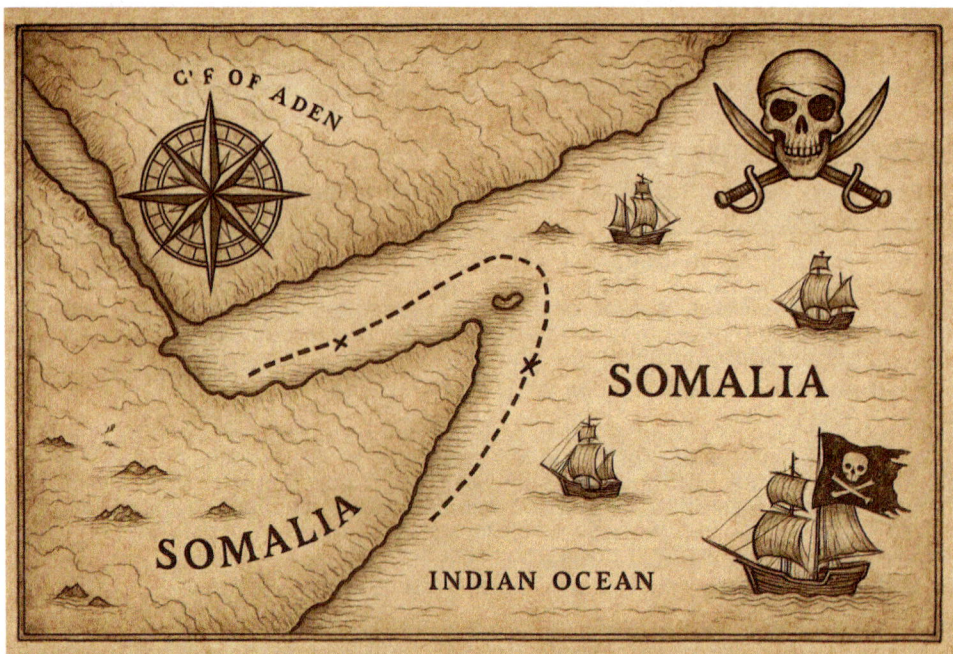

Such dinners were not only for food but also for planning, storytelling, singing, and strengthening brotherhood. Food was a bridge between people — even in pirate life.

9. **Sea provisions: fish in oil and spices in jars.**

To have food during long journeys, Somali pirates preserved fish in oil with pepper and herbs. They placed it in clay jars or metal cans, sealed it, and took it with them. This fish could be eaten with lahoh or simply with a spoon. It was a survival strategy and an example of maritime thinking — always have a reserve!

10. **Somali pirate cuisine — spices, the sea, and the soul of the desert.**

Somali pirate cuisine combines Indian spices, Arab influences, and African simplicity. It is spicy, aromatic, nutritious, and always with a sea accent. Eating like a Somali pirate means appreciating food, sharing it, and staying strong even on the waves. Because a true pirate knows: a full stomach is half the victory.

The culinary world of Somali pirates is a tale of spices, fish aromas, and shared strength. Their dishes are simple but with character, just like the pirates themselves. They teach us that even in the most challenging conditions, you can eat deliciously, with soul and gratitude. And that the greatest treasure is the dinner you share with friends.

Shuro with Smoked Fish: Pirate Soup from East Africa!

1. **Yo-ho-ho! Sailing to the African coast!**

Pirates didn't just sail the Caribbean Sea! Some brave captains navigated the waters of the Indian Ocean near Somalia, where in the hot ports they prepared shuro — a thick, aromatic soup made from chickpea flour, onions, oil, spices, and of course, fish. Today, we will prepare this soup using a pirate recipe. But don't forget — in the kitchen, just like on a ship, there are safety rules. Ask an adult helper to assist with the hot pot and knife.

2. Preparing the ingredients — a culinary treasure chest.

Here's what you need for one large pirate portion:
— 4 tablespoons of chickpea flour (can be found in supermarkets or made from chickpeas in a blender)
— 1 medium onion
— 2 tablespoons of vegetable oil
— 1 teaspoon of turmeric
— 1/2 teaspoon of ground cumin
— a pinch of pepper or paprika
— salt — to taste
— 3 cups of water
— a few pieces of smoked fish (mackerel is ideal)
— greens for serving (cilantro or parsley)

3. Schooner in the pot — making the base with chickpea flour.

In a large bowl, mix the flour with a little cold water (about half a cup) to get a smooth mass without lumps. This will be our "pirate liquid armor," which will make the shuro thick. A little tip: stir with a spoon in one direction, like turning a ship's wheel — then there will be no lumps!

4. Onion — like a caramel treasure in the depths of the soup.

Ask an adult to finely chop the onion, like golden coins. Fry it in a pan with oil until golden. When a sweet smell appears — it's time to add the spices: turmeric, cumin, paprika. Mix everything so that the aroma fills your galley!

5. Combining the bases — starting to cook the soup.

Pour the water into a pot, place it on the stove. When the water boils, carefully add the fried onion with spices. Then slowly pour in the diluted chickpea flour, stirring with a spoon. Cook on low heat, as if brewing a potion in a wizard's cabin!

6. Adding smoked fish — the aroma of a pirate's dock.

Cut the smoked fish into small pieces (an adult will help, as there may be bones!) and throw it into the soup. Cook together for another 5-7 minutes

The fish will add the aroma of smoke and sea adventures. If the soup is too thick — add a little more water, like a real ship adding sails in a storm!

7. Time to taste — but first, let it cool.

Remove the soup from the heat and let it cool a bit. Shuro has a texture like puree — soft, slightly nutty thanks to the chickpeas. Taste with a spoon, not greedily — this soup is worthy of a respectable pirate!

8. Serving — like a feast in the port of Mogadishu.

Pour the shuro into a deep plate, garnish with greens on top. Serve with a piece of bread or flatbread — to dip and eat everything to the last drop. It's like sweeping the treasury to a shine!

9. Tips from the kitchen captain.

— If you don't have chickpea flour, you can make it yourself: grind dry chickpeas in a blender and sift.
— Fish can be replaced with boiled or fried — if you don't like the smoky taste.
— Add a little lemon juice — pirates believed it protected against scurvy!

10. Warning, young culinary corsair!

The stove is hot, the knife is sharp, the fish may have bones. Therefore, all these tasks are for an adult helper. You are the captain of taste, your task is to focus on stirring, seasoning, and serving.

Here it is — pirate shuro with smoked fish, thick, aromatic, and warming, like the sands of the Somali coast.

As you savor it spoon by spoon, imagine how after a storm your pirates gather around the fire, share funny stories, and dream of new adventures.

Fish Shurba: Aromatic Pirate Soup from the Depths of Somalia

1. Sails on the horizon! Time to cook pirate shurba!

Young captain, today you will get acquainted with another treasure of Somali cuisine — fish *shurba*. It's not just a soup, but a true soulful broth for sailors! It differs from *shuro* in that *shurba is more liquid*, with a higher content of vegetables, spicy broth, and pieces of fish. Shuro is thicker, like cream, while shurba is light, like an ocean breeze. So, get ready for a new culinary journey — don't forget to call an adult helper!

2. Ingredients — treasures from the holds of East African ships.

We will need:
— 300 g fish fillet (dorado, hake, or tilapia will do)
— 1 onion
— 2 tomatoes
— 2 cloves of garlic
— 1 carrot
— 1 potato
— 1 teaspoon turmeric
— 1/2 teaspoon cinnamon (a secret pirate ingredient!)
— 1/2 teaspoon ground ginger
— salt, pepper — to taste
— a few sprigs of parsley or cilantro
— 2 tablespoons oil
— 1.5 liters of water or fish broth
— lemon or lime for serving

3. We start with frying — like lighting a fire on the shore.

Ask an adult to finely chop the onion, tomatoes, garlic, carrot, and potato. Heat the oil in a large cauldron or pot. First, fry the onion until golden — like the sun in the desert, then add the garlic, carrot, and tomatoes. Stir like a real ship's cook!

4. **Spice treasure — the true spirit of Somalia.**

Add turmeric, ginger, and a pinch of cinnamon. Yes, cinnamon! In Somalia, they even add it to soup — it gives a warm, sweet aroma, like the smell of a wooden deck under a tropical rain. Fry everything together for a few more minutes.

5. **Add water — the shurba cooking begins.**

Add water or fish broth. Add the potato. Salt, pepper — and let the shurba cook over medium heat for about 15 minutes. The potato should become soft, and the broth aromatic, like spices in a pirate's pouch.

6. **Add the fish — the main star of the soup.**

Cut the fish into small pieces. If there is skin or bones, ask an adult to remove them. Put the fish in the soup and cook for another 10 minutes until it becomes tender. If the fish falls apart — that's good, it gives its flavor to the broth.

7. **Serving nuances — like in a port tavern in Berbera.**

The ready shurba is served hot. Sprinkle fresh herbs on top. Be sure to add a slice of lemon or lime — Somali pirates always had citrus with them to keep the soup fresh and spicy. It can be served with flatbread or boiled rice.

8. **Secrets from the captain-cook.**

— To make the shurba even tastier, let it sit for 10 minutes before serving.
— If you don't like pieces of vegetables, you can blend everything into a cream — then you'll get a pirate "shuro-shurba"!
— Tomatoes can be replaced with tomato puree — if you're in a hurry for a new culinary battle!

9. **How does shurba differ from shuro?**

Shurba is a *liquid soup* with pieces of fish, vegetables, and a lot of spicy broth. *Shuro* is a *thick soup*, almost like porridge, based on chickpea flour and oil. Shurba is light and fresh, shuro is hearty and nutritious. Both dishes were loved by pirates, but they ate them in different weather: shurba in the heat, shuro when it was cool or after a hard raid!

10. Warnings — because even a kitchen cauldron can have a storm.

Hot water and boiling soup are not toys. Ask an adult to pour water, cook, and cut the fish. Your mission is to stir, add spices, decorate, and — most importantly — taste! Like a true navigator, steer the flavor, not the stove!

Your shurba is ready — warm, spicy, like the sands of Somalia, and fresh, like the morning wind over the Indian Ocean.

Fried Tuna with Bananas: An Unexpected Treasure of Somali Pirates!

1. Hey, Captain! Let's sail to a taste surprise!

Today's culinary adventure is for true sea explorers. We are cooking something unusual but very tasty — *fried tuna with bananas*! In Somalia, such a dish is not a rarity but part of the tropical heritage. Here, fish is often served with something sweet because the heat and spices demand freshness and energy. But remember: the kitchen stove is the fire of a pirate ship. Don't set sail without an adult helper!

2. Preparing the ingredients — gathering the tropical catch.

Here are the treasures we need:
— 2 pieces of tuna fillet (can be replaced with hake or mackerel)
— 2 ripe bananas (but not too soft!)
— juice of half a lime or lemon
— 2 cloves of garlic
— salt, black pepper
— 1/2 teaspoon of turmeric
— 2 tablespoons of oil for frying
— greens or lettuce leaves for serving

3. Marinating the fish — a sea captain doesn't eat bland food!

Ask an adult to cut the tuna into convenient pieces. Sprinkle with salt, pepper, turmeric, then rub with minced garlic and drizzle with lime juice. Leave for 10-15 minutes while we prepare the bananas. This marinade is like ship's rum: it gives strength and character!

4. Preparing the bananas — like sweet coins from a tropical island.

Peel the bananas and cut them diagonally into thick slices (so they don't fall apart). This will be the pirate garnish — sweet, soft, with hints of caramel. In Somalia, bananas are often fried with fish or meat — it's a favorite contrasting taste!

5. Frying the tuna — the pan blazes like a battle in the port.

Pour some oil into the pan and heat it. When it becomes hot (but not smoking!), carefully place the fish pieces. Fry for 2-3 minutes on each side. The heat should be medium — don't overcook, as the tuna can become dry. Ask an adult to help with flipping!

6. It's the bananas' turn — the pirate's sweet garnish!

Add a little more oil to the same pan (or use another one). Fry the banana slices for 1-2 minutes on each side until golden brown. They should be golden, like a chest of gold, but not too soft!

7. Assembling the dish — like a treasure map.

Place lettuce leaves or greens on a plate (the pirate background), top with tuna pieces, and next to or on top — fried bananas. Want some spiciness? Sprinkle a little black pepper on top — in Somali ports, they love it spicy!

8. Secrets of taste — from a wise chef in Mogadishu.

— The riper the bananas, the sweeter, but not overripe — otherwise, they will fall apart in the pan.

— It's better not to overcook the fish — tuna is especially tasty when it retains a bit of juiciness.

— You can add a pinch of cinnamon to the bananas during frying — it's a pirate trick!

9. **Warnings, like before a storm!**

The pan is hot, the oil can splatter — so an adult should do the frying or help you. You are in charge of spices, presentation, and tasting! And don't touch the pan with your hands, even if it seems "not very hot."

10. **Bon appétit, Captain! Feel the taste of the Somali coast.**

When you taste the combination of salty tuna and sweet banana, you'll understand why Somali pirates loved such food. It gives energy for journeys, warms the soul, and surprises the taste buds. This taste is like the ocean wind and the warmth of the tropical sun in one spoon.

Fried tuna with bananas is not just a dish, but a pirate skill of combining the unexpected!

Every cook is a bit of a magician, a bit of a traveler, and in our "Pirate Kitchen," also a bit of a captain. To new adventures, sailor!

Somali Fish Curry: A Spicy Storm in a Bowl!

1. **Yo-ho-ho! Pirate curry on the horizon!**

Today we set sail on a culinary voyage through the spicy waters of Somalia! We're making *fish curry* — a spicy, aromatic dish that Somali sailors often cooked in their pots after a successful catch. This dish has character: a bit of fire, lots of flavor, and tender pieces of fish. Don't forget, captain: the kitchen is your deck, but with an adult helper at the helm!

2. **Gathering supplies — treasures of spices and gifts of the sea.**

Here's what you need to prepare:
— 300 g of white fish fillet (such as tilapia or hake)
— 1 onion
— 2 tomatoes or 3 tbsp of tomato paste
— 2 cloves of garlic
— 1 tsp of grated ginger
— 1/2 tsp of turmeric
— 1/2 tsp of ground cumin
— 1/2 tsp of ground coriander
— 1/4 tsp of chili pepper (optional)
— 200 ml of coconut milk or water
— 2 tbsp of vegetable oil
— salt, pepper
— fresh cilantro or parsley for garnish
— rice or flatbreads for serving

3. **Preparing the spices — like alchemists in the galley.**

Ask an adult to chop the onion, garlic, and tomatoes. Heat the oil in a pot or deep pan. First, fry the onion until golden — when it becomes soft, add the garlic and ginger. Stir — the aroma should be as if the ship has just arrived at the spice port!

4. **Time to add the spices — the captain of flavor gives the command!**

Mix in the turmeric, cumin, coriander, and (if desired) a pinch of chili. Fry everything together for another 30 seconds to let the spices "bloom." In Somalia, spices are more than just flavor: they are the smell of home, the sound of laughter in the mess hall, and the songs of the wind!

5. **Tomatoes or paste — adding a rosy sauce.**

Add the chopped tomatoes (or paste) to the spices. Simmer for 5 minutes until the mixture becomes thick, like a treasure map. Add salt, a bit of pepper, and a little water to keep the sauce from being dry.

6. Fish in the sauce — the main star of the curry.

Cut the fish into medium pieces. Carefully place them in the sauce. Pour in coconut milk or water to cover the fish. Cover with a lid and simmer for 10–12 minutes on low heat — until the fish becomes tender, like waves in calm weather.

7. Serving — like a seaside celebration.

Place the ready curry in a bowl or on a plate, sprinkle with chopped cilantro or parsley. Serve with boiled rice or Somali flatbread (which resembles a pancake). In Somalia, they say: "Curry without bread is like a ship without sails!"

8. Secrets from the Somali cook.

— To make the curry creamy, be sure to add coconut milk.
— Want a milder taste? Replace chili with a bit of honey.
— It's better to grate garlic and ginger rather than just chop them — this way, there's more aroma.
— If the fish falls apart, don't worry! In curry, that's normal.

9. Careful, young chef!

Spices don't bite, but hot oil sure does! An adult should do the frying and pouring of water. Don't touch the pan with your hands. You control the flavor and garnishes — and in this, you are a true pirate captain!

10. The taste of victory — like after a good raid!

When you taste the first spoonful of fish curry, imagine: you're sitting on a sandy shore, the waves gently whisper, and your crew is laughing and thanking you for the meal. In Somalia, food is part of hospitality, family warmth, and the magic of spices.

Somali Fish Curry is a spicy adventure in every spoonful.

It teaches us that even the simplest ingredients can become a tale if you add heart, spices, and a bit of pirate courage. Until the next journey, captain!

Fish on Rice "Basbas": A Pirate's Lunch with the Spirit of Somalia!

1. Ahoy, Captain! Let's prepare "basbas" — rice with fish, just like real pirates!

Today we are making *basbas* — not just a word, but a magical name for a dish with fish, rice, and a very fragrant sauce. In Somalia, "basbas" often means something spicy or piquant. So get ready: it will be hot, delicious, and very maritime! Also, ask an adult helper to be nearby, as real culinary storms can happen in the kitchen.

2. Treasures from the stash — ingredients for the marinade and the dish.

Here's what we need:
— 2 pieces of fish fillet (such as tilapia, tuna, or hake)
— 1 tsp turmeric
— 1/2 tsp ground cumin
— 1 clove of garlic (minced)
— juice of 1/2 lemon or lime
— salt and pepper to taste
— 1 cup long-grain rice
— 1 onion
— 2 tomatoes or 2 tbsp tomato paste
— 2 tbsp oil
— 2 cups water or broth
— greens for serving

3. Marinating the fish — like real chefs on the ocean shore.

Cut the fish fillet into large pieces. In a bowl, mix lemon juice, turmeric, cumin, garlic, salt, and pepper. Sprinkle the fish with this marinade, gently coat the pieces, cover, and place in the refrigerator for 20–30 minutes. In Somali villages, it is believed that well-marinated fish "absorbs the sun and wind"!

4. Starting with the rice — the base for a ship's dinner.

Rinse the rice thoroughly several times until the water is clear. Then soak it in cold water for 10–15 minutes — this will make it fluffy and light, like sand on the shore. Meanwhile, let's start preparing the other ingredients.

5. Preparing the sauce — the heart of the "basbas" dish.

In a deep frying pan or pot, heat 1 tbsp of oil. Add finely chopped onion and fry until soft. Then add tomatoes or tomato paste and a little salt. Let the vegetables become soft until they turn into a spicy, aromatic sauce.

6. Frying the fish — after marinating, it's ready for a culinary battle!

In a separate pan, heat the remaining oil. Carefully place the marinated fish and fry for 2–3 minutes on each side until golden brown. Ask an adult to help to avoid hot splashes. The fish already has a bright aroma of spices — like a real pirate!

7. Cooking the rice with the sauce — like brewing storms in a pot.

Add the rice to the vegetable sauce, pour in 2 cups of water or broth, and add a little salt. Stir, bring to a boil, reduce the heat, and cover with a lid. Cook for 15–20 minutes until the rice absorbs all the liquid. Do not open the lid often — let the rice steam like a sail!

8. The finale — combining fish and rice in harmony of taste.

When the rice is ready, carefully place the fried fish on top. Cover and leave for 5 minutes to let everything "befriend." The aromas will mix like pirate fleets before a victory feast!

9. **Serving — like at a royal pirate banquet.**

Place the rice on a large plate, top with juicy pieces of fish. Garnish with greens, you can add lime wedges. Serve with pita, flatbread, or yogurt sauce — this will help soften the spiciness if a "spicy storm" starts in your mouth.

10. **Tips and warnings from the culinary captain:**

— Do not marinate the fish for more than an hour — it will become too soft.
— If you don't like spicy food, don't add chili; basbas will still be delicious.
— Be careful with hot oil and steam! Do not fry or open the lid without adult help.
— Always wash your hands after marinating fish — like a real boatswain after a hard watch.

Here is your fish on rice "basbas" — a dish worthy of a pirate's treasure.

It combines the sea, spices, and the warmth of the Somali shores in every spoonful. Cook with soul, Captain, because real cooking is also an adventure! To new flavors and new seas!

Maalwa and Stewed Vegetables: A Pirate's Breakfast from Somalia!

1. **Good morning, Captain! It's time for a pirate's breakfast!**

On the east coast of Africa, near the shores of Somalia, pirates would start their day with *maalwa* — sweet pancakes with the aromas of cardamom and cinnamon. They were often served with *stewed vegetables* to provide strength for a day of adventures. So prepare your culinary map — we're setting sail on a delicious voyage! But first — an adult helper in the galley is a must!

Preparing Maalwa (Somali Pancakes)

2. **Ingredients — like treasures from a tropical market:**

— 1 cup of flour
— 1 egg
— 1 cup of milk (or water)
— 2 tablespoons of sugar
— 1/2 teaspoon of cinnamon
— 1/2 teaspoon of ground cardamom
— a pinch of salt
— 1/2 teaspoon of baking soda or baking powder
— oil for frying

3. **Kneading the dough — like mixing wind and spices.**

In a large bowl, mix all the dry ingredients: flour, spices, sugar, salt, and soda. Then add the egg and milk. Stir with a whisk or spoon to avoid lumps. The batter should be slightly thicker than regular pancake batter. Let it "rest" for 5–10 minutes while you prepare the vegetables.

4. **Frying the maalwa — on the pan, like on a hot deck!**

Heat a pan with a drop of oil. Pour a little batter and gently spread it with a spoon. Maalwa should be a bit fluffy, like a pancake. Fry for 1–2 minutes on each side. When bubbles appear, it's time to flip. Don't make them too thin — pirates love hearty meals!

Stewed Vegetables — like a side dish from the island's mess hall

5. **Ingredients — bright treasures of the earth:**

— 1 carrot
— 1 potato
— 1/2 onion
— a few pieces of cabbage or zucchini
— 1 clove of garlic
— 1/2 teaspoon of turmeric
— salt, pepper
— 1 tablespoon of oil
— 1/2 cup of water

6. **Preparing the vegetables — like sorting jewels.**

Ask an adult to cut the vegetables into small pieces. Carrot — into rounds, potato — into cubes, cabbage — into strips. Finely grate or chop the garlic. Everything is ready for stewing!

7. **Cooking the vegetables — stewing in a spiced lagoon.**

In a pan or pot, heat the oil. Sauté the onion and garlic until soft. Add turmeric — it will make the vegetables golden, like treasure. Then toss in all the vegetables, add salt, pepper, and water. Cover with a lid and stew for 15 minutes on low heat until everything is soft but not mushy.

Serving — like a celebration after a successful raid

8. **Serving the pirate feast.**

Place 1–2 maalwa pancakes on a plate, alongside a few spoonfuls of vegetables. You can roll the maalwa and dip it into the vegetables — pirates ate with their hands! For a sweet version of maalwa, you can add a spoonful of honey or date syrup on top.

9. **Secrets of the pirate's cabin:**

— Add grated apple or banana to the batter for a fruity maalwa!
— You can toss in a bit of cooked beans or peas into the vegetables for variety.
— If there's leftover maalwa, you can fry it again the next day and eat it with butter!

10. **A safe galley — the key to a good meal!**

The pan and steam are like real fire in a storm! So an adult should do the frying. You can stir, mix ingredients, and garnish the dish. When everything is ready — it's time to call the crew to the table!

Maalwa and stewed vegetables — morning strength for little explorers of the world!

It's not just breakfast — it's a tradition. Somali families gather around such a table, share stories, and savor every bite. Are you ready for the next adventure?

Somali Shaai: The Hot Tea of the Pirates of the Desert and Ocean!

1. **Yo-ho-ho, let's brew tea like real pirates from Africa!**

Today we are not frying, boiling, or stewing. We are making *shaai* — hot Somali tea with cardamom, ginger, and sugar. Somali pirates drank it after a hard sail or in the morning before a raid — to wake up and warm up. Such tea is not just a drink, but a magical potion of strength and hospitality. But remember, the kettle is not a shell, it's hot! Call an adult helper to make sure everything goes safely.

2. **Ingredients — treasures from the eastern market.**

To make 2 pirate cups of tea, you need:
— 2 cups of water
— 2 teaspoons of black tea (preferably loose) or 2 tea bags
— 2–3 cardamom pods
— 1 slice of fresh ginger (can be grated)
— 2–3 tablespoons of sugar (Somalis love it very sweet!)
— 1/4 cup of milk (more if desired)

3. **Let's start boiling — the pirate's tea kettle is boiling!**

Pour water into a saucepan or small kettle. Add crushed cardamom (ask an adult to slightly crush the pods with a spoon) and a slice of ginger. Turn on the stove (with an adult!) and bring to a boil. The water should bubble — this means the spices have awakened!

4. **Add the tea — a potion of strength and calm.**

When the water has been boiling for 2–3 minutes, add the tea. If it's tea bags, just throw them in the water. If loose, pour it directly. Reduce the heat and simmer for another 3 minutes. The color will become darker, the aroma stronger. This is not just tea — it's a tea storm!

5. **Sugar! The sweetness loved by Somali pirates.**

Add 2–3 tablespoons of sugar (even more if you like!). Somalis say: if the spoon stands in the tea, it's sweet enough. Stir everything carefully. Sweet tea gives energy after a night watch!

6. **Add milk — a cloud in a pirate's cup.**

Pour in a little milk. The tea will turn a caramel color — warm like the sand by the ocean. Don't overpour — the tea should remain strong, not turn into milk with a hint of tea!

7. **Strain — no tea splinters in the captain's cup!**

Ask an adult to strain the tea through a sieve into a teapot or directly into cups. Be careful — it's hot, like a ship after a battle! Stay away from the kettle's spout.

8. **Time to drink — with respect, as in a Somali port.**

Tea is drunk in small sips, often with bread, flatbread, or dates. In Somalia, it is served to guests as a sign of respect. Sit quietly, thank your helper, and imagine you're on a veranda by the sea, listening to the songs of seagulls and laughing with the crew.

9. **Secrets from the tea captain.**

— If there's no fresh ginger, you can use dried (a pinch).
— Want it more aromatic? Add a cinnamon stick or clove.
— In Somalia, there is both black shaai and white (with a lot of milk). Choose the one you like!

10. **Warnings, like in a storm!**

The tea is hot, like the tropical sun! Never pour it yourself without adult help. The kettle, stove, boiling water — these are serious things. But adding spices, stirring sugar, and decorating the cup — that's your job, captain!

Somali shaai is not just a drink, it's a piece of distant culture and the spirit of adventure.

It warms, unites, and inspires. Drink slowly, with a smile, and prepare for the next culinary battle — there are still so many flavors of oceans and deserts ahead!

Halva with Spices: The Sweet Treasure of Somali Pirates!

1. **Hey-hey, sweet winds in the face! Today we are making halva!**

Young captain, today your galley will turn into a magical workshop. We will prepare *Somali halva with spices* — thick, aromatic, and chewy, like a real caramel journey. In Somalia, this halva is made for holidays, weddings, and... after successful sea raids! But be careful: sugar is not a toy, but a hot avalanche. Everything related to the stove should be done with an adult helper!

2. **Treasures from the hold: here's what we need.**

To prepare a small pirate portion:
— 1 cup of sugar
— 1/2 cup of water
— 2 tablespoons of corn or potato starch
— 1/4 cup of oil (preferably odorless)
— 1/2 teaspoon of ground cinnamon
— 1/4 teaspoon of ground cardamom
— a pinch of ground ginger
— a pinch of salt
— optionally — a handful of roasted nuts or seeds

3. **Preparing spices — like a pirate's potion for luck.**

In a small bowl, mix cinnamon, cardamom, ginger, and a pinch of salt. This will be our "magic powder." In Somalia, spices are the heart of halva. Their aroma reminds of caravans, sand, and markets near the Indian Ocean!

4. **Cooking syrup — like melting gold!**

Pour sugar and water into a saucepan with a thick bottom. Turn on the stove (only with an adult!) and stir until the sugar dissolves. When the syrup starts to boil — don't touch it with your hands! It's very hot. In Somalia, halva is cooked on a high flame, but we will make it carefully and wisely.

5. **Adding starch — the thickness of the treasure.**

In a separate bowl, dissolve the starch in a few tablespoons of cold water. When the syrup boils for 2–3 minutes, slowly pour in the starch mixture, stirring constantly with a spoon. The magical transformation begins: the liquid will become thick, shiny — like a freshly unearthed treasure!

6. **Pouring in oil and adding spices.**

Gradually add oil, stirring — it will make the halva elastic. Then add our spices. Continue stirring until the mixture becomes thick and it's hard to turn the spoon. If you want — add some roasted nuts (like pirate trophies!)

7. Placing halva in a mold — an island in a caramel sea.

Ask an adult to line the mold with parchment or grease it with oil. Pour the hot halva and smooth it with a spoon. Be careful — don't touch the halva with your hands, it can burn! Let it cool for 30 minutes.

8. Cutting when it hardens — like dividing the loot.

When the halva hardens and becomes firm, cut it into squares or diamonds — like pirate coins. Serve on a plate with a pinch of cinnamon on top. In Somalia, it's eaten with a glass of hot chai or simply with a smile!

9. Tips from the sweet captain.

— To prevent the halva from sticking in the mold — grease it with oil or line it with paper.
— Instead of water, you can use a bit of juice or even milk — it will be more tender.
— If you want color — add a pinch of turmeric (that's how they do it in Mogadishu!)

10. Careful, helmsman! Halva is hot, like sand at noon.

Hot caramel is very dangerous. Only an adult can pour and stir on the stove. You can be in charge of mixing spices, preparing the mold, cutting after cooling. And, of course, tasting!

Somali halva is not just a sweet treat, it's a piece of history you can hold in your hands.

The taste of spices, the chewiness, the aroma of cinnamon — all this reminds of distant journeys, sea adventures, and warm evenings by the campfire. To new delicious discoveries, captain of the sweet deck!

Fish in Oil with Pepper and Herbs: A Pirate's Way to Preserve the Taste of the Sea!

1. Ahoy, Captain! Let's learn to preserve fish like real pirates!

In ancient times, when there were no refrigerators, pirates and sailors from Somalia preserved fish *in oil with spicy herbs and pepper*. This way, the fish could last for several weeks, remaining tasty and juicy. Today, we will repeat this secret pirate method! But remember: anything involving knives, the stove, or boiling water is the responsibility of an adult helper.

2. What do we put in the pirate jar?

Here are our ingredients:
— 2 pieces of fish fillet (best are mackerel, tuna, hake, or dorado)
— 1 cup of vegetable oil (sunflower or olive)
— 1 teaspoon of salt
— 1/2 teaspoon of black pepper (whole or ground)
— 1 bay leaf
— 2-3 cloves of garlic
— sprigs of rosemary, thyme, or parsley (to taste)
— sterilized glass jar with a lid

3. Preparing the fish — getting ready for a long voyage.

Ask an adult to cut the fish into small pieces. Rinse it in water and dry it. You can slightly boil it in salted water (5-6 minutes) or fry it — this way, it will preserve better. Don't forget to cool the fish before placing it in the jar.

4. Pirate treasure in a jar — layering the fish.

Place the pieces of fish in a clean, dry jar in layers. Between them, place garlic, pepper, bay leaf, and herbs. Imagine you're creating a treasure map: everything should be beautiful and tight, leaving no air!

5. **Oil — the magical liquid that protects against time.**

Pour oil over everything — so that it completely covers the fish and spices. If needed, add more. It's like waves covering the shore: nothing should peek out from under the oil!

6. **Closing — sealing the pirate secret.**

Ask an adult to tightly close the jar with a lid. If the jar is hot after sterilization — be careful, don't touch it! Let it cool down. Now this jar is your personal pirate treasure with the taste of the sea!

7. Storage — in the hold or on the shelf?

Store the jar in the refrigerator. The fish will be ready to eat in 1–2 days, but it will be the tastiest in a week! You can make sandwiches, salads, or eat it just with bread. In the holds of pirate ships, such jars were hidden in the coolest places.

8. **Tips from the fish captain.**

— If you want a spicy taste, add a pinch of red pepper or clove.
— Don't overload the jar: air between layers is the enemy of long-term storage.
— Want the smell of the sea? Use a bit of dried seaweed!

9. **Attention, danger on the horizon!**

Hot jar, knives, fish with bones — all of this can be dangerous. Ask an adult to sterilize the jar (pour boiling water over it) and handle the stove. You are in charge of spices, layering, and decoration!

10. **When you open the jar — you'll feel like you're by the sea.**

Somali pirates ate such fish in ports, on the road, and even during night watches. It is rich in flavor, aromatic, and in every piece — a memory of the sea. Taste it — and feel like a true captain of taste and time!

Preserving fish in oil is an art and wisdom that true sailors possessed.

Now you know how to create a little treasure in a jar — and keep a piece of the sea even when it's calm and you're at home. To new adventures, captain of canned treasures!

Somali Fish Patties: Pirate Coins with the Taste of the Ocean!

1. Ahoy, crew! Today we're making pirate patties!

These small round fish patties are a true treasure of Somali ports. They are made in every family: for breakfast, celebrations, or just as a snack after a sea watch. The main thing is lots of flavor and even more heart! But remember: we don't pirate in the kitchen! The stove is serious business. Ask an adult to help with hot and sharp things.

2. Gathering ingredients — like treasures in a sea bag.

We need:
— 1 large boiled potato
— 1/2 cup of cooked or canned fish (tuna, mackerel, hake)
— 1 egg
— 1/2 small onion
— 1 clove of garlic
— 1/4 tsp ground cumin
— 1/4 tsp ground coriander
— salt and pepper to taste
— herbs (parsley or cilantro)
— breadcrumbs or flour
— oil for frying

3. Preparing the base — a mixture like a pirate legend!

Mash the potato with a fork in a bowl — it should be soft like beach sand. Add the chopped fish to it. If there are bones, ask an adult to remove them. Then add finely chopped onion, crushed garlic, spices, salt, and pepper. Mix everything well!

4. Adding the egg — so the mixture is like a united crew.

Crack the egg into the bowl (carefully!) and mix everything together again. The mixture should be soft, slightly sticky, but not runny. If it falls apart, add some breadcrumbs or flour. Pirates always had backup tricks for culinary storms!

5. Forming the patties — golden coins for the crew!

Wet your hands with water and form small circles — thick like two coins together. Roll them in breadcrumbs or flour to make them crispy. Place them on a plate — as if preparing a treasure for the chief captain.

6. Frying with caution — oil like the scorching sun of Somalia.

Heat a little oil in a pan (an adult will help). Carefully place the patties and fry for 2-3 minutes on each side. They should become golden, like tanned pirates after a raid. Carefully flip them with a spatula — don't rush, and everything will be delicious!

7. Serving — a true feast on the deck!

Place the patties on a paper towel to remove excess oil. Serve with yogurt sauce, ketchup, or fresh vegetables. Somalis love to eat them with flatbread — as a snack with tea or a meal on the go.

8. Flavor secrets — from the captain of the culinary fleet.

— Want some heat? Add a pinch of ground chili or a tiny piece of pepper.
— No egg? Add more potatoes or some crushed oats.
— Don't want to fry? Try baking in the oven (but you'll need an adult's help here too!).

9. **Careful, navigator!**

Hot pan, oil, knives — all require caution. Never put patties in hot oil by yourself. An adult helps with frying, and you prepare the mixture, form the patties, serve, and — most importantly — taste!

10. **Bon appétit, captain! You did it!**

Somali fish patties are not just a snack. They are a piece of the culture of a people who live by the ocean, know the taste of fish, and appreciate every spice. And now you are part of this legend too. Enjoy! To new taste expeditions!

Somali fish patties — simple, delicious, with character, like a true sailor.

They are made not for show, but for the soul — and in every bite, you can feel the salty sea, the warm wind, and the joy of a shared meal. Are you ready for the next culinary journey? The pirate kitchen awaits!

Banana Pilaf with Fish: The Captain's Tropical Lunch!

1. **Yo-ho-ho! Today we're cooking a real tropical pilaf!**

In Somalia, pilaf is not just a dish, it's a festive song in a pan! And it's also a simple and delicious way to feed the whole crew after a sea crossing. But we'll make a *pirate version*: with bananas and fish. Is this combination strange? Not at all! In Somalia, they love it this way: salty, sweet, and tropical — all together, like a real adventure. But be careful: the pan is as hot as the desert sun. An adult helper is a must!

2. **Treasures from the Hold: What We Need**

Ingredients for 2–3 servings:
— 1 cup of long-grain rice (e.

g. , basmati)
— 1 medium fish or 2 pieces of fillet (tuna, mackerel, hake)
— 1 ripe but not soft banana
— 1 small onion
— 1/2 tsp turmeric
— 1/2 tsp ground cumin
— salt and pepper to taste
— 2 tablespoons of oil
— 2 cups of water
— a few parsley or cilantro leaves (optional)

3. **We start with the fish — the main character of the tropical pilaf.**

Ask an adult to cut the fish into pieces and remove all the bones. Salt, pepper, and add a pinch of turmeric. Fry in a pan with a little oil — 2–3 minutes on each side. Place the cooked fish on a plate, but don't wash the pan — you'll need it again!

4. **Onion and spices — smoke from the galley!**

In the same pan, fry the chopped onion until golden. Add cumin and a little more turmeric. This is the base of our "pilaf treasure" — an aroma that fills the kitchen like sailors' songs in the night silence.

5. **Time for rice — the base of the pirate lunch.**

Rinse the rice thoroughly (several times until the water is clear). Add it to the onion with spices. Mix everything so the rice absorbs the aroma. This is called "sautéing" — like warming up before a real voyage!

6. **Add water — set course for readiness!**

Pour water over the rice, add salt, and bring to a boil. Reduce the heat, cover with a lid, and cook for 10–15 minutes until the water is absorbed. Make sure nothing burns — on a pirate ship, all food is as precious as gold!

7. **Time for bananas — a sweet surprise in the hold!**

Peel the banana and cut it into slices. When the rice is almost ready, gently mix in the banana slices and pieces of cooked fish

Cover and leave for 5 minutes on very low heat or just under the lid — let the dish "come together" like a ship reaching the harbor.

8. Serving — like in the port of Berbera after a long journey.

Place the banana-fish pilaf on a plate, garnish with greens. You can add a slice of lemon on the side for freshness. In Somalia, such pilaf is often served with a glass of warm tea.

9. Tips from the chef of the eastern coast:

— Don't use overripe bananas — they will fall apart in the pilaf.
— Want more color? Add grated carrot or peas.
— Fish holds its shape better if fried separately rather than cooked with rice.

10. Be careful, young pirate!

The stove, pan, hot oil — all of this is dangerous. An adult should help with frying and cooking. You are the chef for selecting spices, rinsing rice, serving, and, of course, the best tasting!

Banana pilaf with fish — an unexpected but incredibly delicious adventure!

In every spoonful — the salty taste of the sea, the sweetness of the banana, and the spicy spirit of spices. This is how Somali pirates ate: mixing the simplest into something unforgettable. To new taste discoveries, captain of the culinary ship!

Malabar Pirates

1. Breakfast in the Coconut Harbor: Idiyappam and Fish Curry.

The Malabar pirates from the coast of Kerala (India) started their day with a delicious and unusual dish — idiyappam, or rice "noodle-cakes," steamed to perfection. They were served with fish curry, aromatic and not too spicy for the morning. The dishes were dominated by coconut, curry leaves, and mustard seeds. The aromas of spices awakened them as effectively as the ringing of a ship's bell. They drank black tea with cardamom or fresh coconut juice.

2. Fish Soup "Meen Kalan" — the rich bounty of the sea.

For lunch, the pirates chose the rich soup "Meen Kalan" — a thick broth with a tangy flavor, made with tamarind, coconut milk, and fried sea fish. Spices were added to enhance the ocean's taste: turmeric, fennel, asafoetida. This soup not only warmed them after the rain but also provided energy before a new raid — the key was to eat it hot and with lahi (a thin flatbread).

3. Main Dish: Fish in Banana Leaf — "Meen Pollichathu".

As the day turned to evening, the pirate fires cooked "Meen Pollichathu" — fish marinated in spices, wrapped in banana leaves, and grilled over coals. The fish was chosen based on availability — usually carp or tuna. Inside the leaves, the juice, aroma, and tender texture were preserved. It was a festive end to any day, especially after a successful sea voyage.

4. Side Dishes: Lemon Rice and Stewed Vegetables with Coconut.

Side dishes were an important part of the Malabar meal. Lemon rice was served with the fish — rice fried with mustard seeds, peanuts, curry leaves, and fresh lime juice. They also often prepared "thoran" — a vegetable stew with cabbage, carrots, or beans, seasoned with grated coconut and mustard seeds. This added color and textural contrast to the fish base.

5. Sea Snack: Fried Squid "Koonthal Fry".

The pirates loved crunchy snacks that were easy to prepare right on the ship. "Koonthal Fry" — fried squid in a dry marinade of red pepper, garlic, and lime juice. They were fried to a crispy crust, making it the perfect dish for a quick snack or a communal dinner with the whole crew by the shore.

6. **Beverages: Coconut Water and Salty "Sea" Lassi.**

In the tropics, one must drink a lot. The favorite drink of the Malabar pirates was water from a young coconut — sweet, refreshing, and natural. They also drank salty lassi — a yogurt drink with cumin and salt, which cooled, refreshed, and improved digestion after spicy dishes. They also prepared a drink with panang kalkandu — palm sugar dissolved in water with lemon.

7. **Desserts: Banana "Unniyappam" and Sweet Rice Pudding.**

For dessert — warm "unniyappam": pancake-balls made from rice flour, bananas, coconut, and cardamom. They were fried in coconut oil to a golden crust. Another sweet treasure — "payasam" (rice pudding in coconut milk with pieces of cashew nuts and raisins). These treats lasted several days and were a favorite trophy after battles and trade.

8. **The Tradition of Communal Meals — an Anchor for the Crew.**

The Malabar pirates valued unity. In the evenings, they gathered around a large banana leaf, which served as a plate, and ate together with their hands — it tasted better that way! The food was not only for nourishment but also for bonding. Conversations, plans, jokes — everything merged into a single pirate atmosphere. Even newcomers felt like part of the family after such a dinner.

9. **Supplies for the Ship: Fish Paste and Fried Rice Cakes.**

Pirates had to take food with them on voyages. Fish paste (like "meen chutney") — dried fish with pepper and tamarind — was stored in clay jars. They also prepared fried rice cakes "ada," which stayed fresh for several days. This was convenient and hearty food that could be quickly eaten during sea adventures or dangerous maneuvers.

10. **Malabar Cuisine — an Exotic Journey in Every Bite.**

The cuisine of the Malabar pirates is a blend of Arabic, Indian, and Portuguese influences. It smells of coconut, sounds of curry leaves, and burns with the fire of spices. Fish dishes here are not just food but stories of the sea, trade, travels, and family. They tell of people who lived at the crossroads of oceans and cultures and knew how to turn any meal into a culinary fairy tale.

Malabar cuisine is not just the diet of pirates but a true map of taste, charted between waves, spices, and sails. It teaches us to appreciate simple ingredients, share meals, and enjoy every spoonful — like a true pirate of the Kerala coast. Eating is an adventure too!

Idiyappam: Steamed Threads of Happiness from Malabar!

1. Yo-ho-ho! A Malabar morning begins with idiyappam!

Greetings, young pirate! Today we are preparing a true breakfast of Malabar sea wolves — idiyappam. These are steamed "rice threads" that resemble a magical web woven by the culinary spirits of the tropics. But to create this wonder, you'll need a bit of patience, a pirate's mood, and, of course, an adult helper. Ready? The cauldron is humming — let's begin!

2. The treasure chest of ingredients: seeking tropical grains.

To prepare idiyappam, you will need:
— 1 cup of rice flour (as fine as the sand on the Malabar coast)
— 1 cup of hot water
— a pinch of salt
— grated coconut (optional, but true pirates love it!)

This is all — a simple yet magical formula, like an ancient recipe from a culinary treasure map.

3. Mix the dough — don't overdo it with water!

In a large bowl, pour in the rice flour and salt. Carefully, like a true alchemist, add the hot water. This task is for an adult — the water should be very hot, almost boiling. Stir with a spoon or a dragon spoon (that's what we call a wooden spatula) until you get a soft, elastic dough. It should be like clay — soft but not sticky.

4. Magic bag or vermicelli press.

Here you'll need a special pirate artifact — a *sev press* or idiyappam press (you can buy one or borrow from Indian neighbors). If you don't have one — you can use a pastry syringe with a small opening. Put some dough inside — and start pressing! Thin rice threads will come out, like the beard of an old pirate. :)

5. Steaming — like in the tropical mist.

Arrange the rice threads in circles or fans on parchment or a banana leaf (for a true tropical mood). If you like, sprinkle coconut on top. Then place in a steamer for 7-10 minutes. Don't have a steamer? Ask an adult to place a rack in a pot of water, cover with a lid — it will be an improvised tropical steamboat!

6. Coconut duet: how to make something sweet for idiyappam.

Idiyappam tastes best with coconut milk and sugar or with curry. For a sweet version — mix coconut milk with a bit of cane sugar (can be replaced with honey). It will be a sweet sea for the rice threads!

7. Malabar curry — a spicy friend for a pirate.

If you're brave and love spicy dishes, try it with vegetable or egg curry. In Malabar, pirates often ate idiyappam with a spicy sauce made of coconut, ginger, and green pepper. But be careful — some spices burn like the sun on the deck!

8. Serving — how to present it so the ship applauds.

Arrange the idiyappam in the shape of nests on a plate, garnish with mint leaves or banana slices. If you're serving with coconut milk — serve it in a small bowl on the side. Want to surprise the captain? Top with raisins or mango!

9. Secrets from the Malabar galley.

— It's better to toast the rice flour in a dry pan before mixing — it adds aroma.
— Add water gradually — the dough shouldn't be wet

— If pressing is difficult — lightly oil your hands.
— Idiyappam is delicious even cold, like leftovers for a pirate breakfast the next day!

10. **Careful, young sailor: steam and hot water!**

Never lean over a boiling steamer! The steam can burn. Use kitchen gloves or a towel when opening the lid. And most importantly — don't rush. Idiyappam doesn't like fuss, only calm and pirate respect.

Here it is — your own idiyappam, created with love and steam!

This is not just breakfast — it's the taste of South India, where spices, coconuts, and the spirit of open seas live in every dish. When you eat idiyappam, imagine yourself by a campfire on a Malabar beach, where pirates laugh, and coconuts fall from the palms. Enjoy, captain! The next culinary voyage is already on the horizon!

Fish Soup "Minn Kalan": Spicy Malabar Surf!

1. **Welcome, Captain! It's time to cook Minn Kalan — the pirate's fish elixir!**

Far away on the Malabar coast, where the waves whisper the secrets of spices, pirates brewed a special soup — *Minn Kalan*. This aromatic, slightly tangy fish soup invigorated even the most tired sailors. Today, we will cook it together. But first — safety! Hot fire and sharp spices require an attentive cook and his senior sailor-adult.

2. **Gathering treasures for the soup.**

Here's what you need to find in the holds:
— 300 g of boneless fish (preferably white — cod, tilapia, or dorado)
— 1/2 teaspoon of turmeric
— 1/2 teaspoon of ground pepper (or a pinch for children)
— 1 cup of coconut milk
— 1/2 cup of tamarind water (or lemon juice if there's no tamarind)
— 1 teaspoon of garlic puree
— 1 teaspoon of ginger puree
— 1 green chili (optional!)
— salt, to taste
— a few curry leaves (or bay leaf)
Gathered? Well done! Everything is ready for the magic of the cauldron.

3. **Preparing the fish — like in a pirate fisherman's workshop.**

Ask an adult to clean and cut the fish into large pieces. Rinse them in cold water, pat dry with a napkin. Then sprinkle a little turmeric and salt — this is not only for taste but also as a pirate's armor: it will protect the fish from falling apart in the soup.

4. **Tamarind or lemon — the tang of a pirate's heart.**

If you have tamarind paste — mix a teaspoon in half a cup of warm water. Don't have it? Lemon will come to the rescue. The tang is an important part of Minn Kalan because it makes the soup resemble the sea surf — unexpectedly refreshing!

5. **Preparing the spicy broth.**

Heat a little oil in a pot. Add ginger and garlic, stirring carefully. Then add turmeric, a little pepper (or don't add it — pirate children should be careful with the fire of spices!). Pour in the tamarind water, add curry leaves and salt. Bring to a boil — and the sea of aromas sways!

6. **Time to release the fish into the ocean of broth.**

Carefully place the pieces of fish into the boiling soup. Cook gently — on low heat, so the fish cooks tenderly, as if dozing in a tropical lagoon. About 10 minutes — and it's ready

Don't stir too much — otherwise, the fish will fall apart.

7. Coconut milk — the white gold of Malabar.

Reduce the heat. Add a cup of coconut milk, stir very carefully. Do not boil after this — otherwise, the milk may "get angry" and curdle. It's better to just warm it. Pirates used to say: "The sea winds are gentle if you don't irritate them!"

8. Tasting — a delicious ritual on board.

Taste the soup (careful, it's hot!) — if needed, add more salt or a little lemon. It should be slightly tangy, aromatic, with a creamy coconut trail and the warmth of spices. Congratulations — this is the taste of Malabar!

9. Galley secrets.

— Add the fish only to boiling broth — then it won't fall apart.
— If you're afraid of spiciness, don't add green chili.
— It's better to add coconut milk at the end, don't boil it.
— If possible, use a clay pot — it retains heat and flavor.

10. Caution — the main rule on board!

The soup is very hot, like the summer sand in the port of Kozhikode! Don't try it immediately after cooking. Always use a spoon and a towel when handling the pot. Ask an adult to pour the soup into a bowl. And most importantly — don't rush: every spoonful is like a new wave of a delicious ocean.

Here it is — your Minn Kalan, the soup known to all Malabar pirates!

This is not just a dish — it's a warm story about spices, fish, and the power of the ocean. Every spoonful is like a journey along the coast of India, where palm trees lean over the shore, and cooking is the magic of everyday life. Eat, enjoy, dream of new adventures — and hold your spoon, Captain, there are many more flavors ahead!

Fish in Banana Leaf — «Meen Pollichathu»: An Aromatic Adventure from the Malabar Coast!

1. Ahoy, young captain! Today we are cooking fish in a real banana leaf!

Imagine yourself on the Malabar coast: the sea is roaring, spices are fragrant, and pirates are cooking their favorite dish — *Meen Pollichathu*. This is fish wrapped in a banana leaf and fried so well that even seagulls gather around. Get ready for a culinary journey! But remember: the stove, knife, and spices are not toys. Call an adult helper — your ship's cook!

2. Gathering ingredients for a tropical wonder.

You will need:
— 2 fillets of white fish (such as dorado or tilapia)
— 2 banana leaves (can be replaced with foil, but real pirates use leaves!)
— 1 onion
— 1 tomato
— 1 teaspoon of garlic-ginger paste
— 1/2 teaspoon of turmeric
— 1 teaspoon of paprika or sweet chili
— juice of half a lemon
— salt — to taste
— 2 tablespoons of coconut oil or regular oil

3. Preparing the fish — pirate marination!

Rinse the fish and pat dry. In a separate bowl, mix a little salt, turmeric, lemon juice, and paprika. Rub this marinade all over the fish — it should become as bright as the sun over Kerala. Leave for 10 minutes to let the spices "sail" through the fillet like boats on a lagoon.

4. **Preparing the filling — the aromatic core of the dish.**

Ask an adult to help: chop the onion and tomato. Heat a little oil in a pan, add the garlic-ginger paste, then the onion — fry until it becomes soft like mist over water. Add tomatoes, spices, a little salt. Simmer until you get a fragrant mixture — similar to curry. This is the heart of your fish!

5. **Banana leaves — a natural package for the fish.**

The banana leaf needs to be softened a bit. Ask an adult to press it against a hot pan for a few seconds — it will become flexible like a sail. And if there are no leaves — foil will do. But with leaves — it's tastier and more romantic!

6. **Wrapping — like a real pirate scroll.**

Place the leaf on the table, inside — a little filling, on top — the marinated fish, and on top again — a little of that onion mixture. Wrap the fish like a gift — carefully, tightly. Tie with kitchen string or simply fold the edges like making an envelope.

7. **Frying — sail-like silence on the pan.**

Pirates fried the wrapped fish on a hot stove or even coals! But we'll use a pan. Heat a little oil. Place the fish in the packages and fry for 5 minutes on each side over medium heat. The leaf should darken — that's a good sign. Inside, everything will heat up like in a pirate galley oven.

8. **Unwrapping — the moment of truth!**

Remove the fish from the stove, wait a minute (careful — it's hot!). Now open the package — the aroma of spices and coconut will fill the kitchen like a tropical wind. Everyone nearby will immediately understand — there's a real cook in the galley!

9. **Secrets of Malabar cooking.**

— If you add coconut flakes to the filling — it will be even more authentic!
— The banana leaf gives the dish a special aroma — of the forest, sun, and spices.
— Do not overheat the pan — the leaf may burn. The heat should be gentle, like a song in the port.

10. **Caution on the kitchen deck!**

Hot oil is not water from a sea puddle! Never lean too close to the pan. Always use a spatula, towel, or kitchen tongs. Let an adult check the readiness of the fish — your job is creativity and spices!

That's it, captain — you've created a real Meen Pollichathu!

This is not just food — it's a tropical tale wrapped in a leaf. Each piece is like an adventure: a bit of smoke, a bit of spice, a sea of flavor, and a lot of soul. Now you know the secrets of the old Malabar pirates. Remember — cooking is not just about food, but also about the stories we create together.

Lemon Rice: Yellow Treasure with Lime and Spices!

1. **Ahoy, young sailor! Today we are cooking golden lemon rice from Malabar!**

In distant India, where spices grow like weeds and limes fall from trees straight into the pan, pirates invented a magical dish — *lemon rice*. It is bright yellow, smells of mustard seeds, and has a crunchy surprise — peanuts! Let's cook it together — but remember: the pan, hot oil, and spices require attention. Call an adult senior sailor and take the culinary helm!

2. **Ingredients — the gold of the pirate's galley.**

Find in your holds:
— 1 cup of cooked rice (best if cooled)
— 2 tablespoons of peanuts (unsalted)
— 1 teaspoon of mustard seeds
— 1 teaspoon of turmeric
— 6–8 curry leaves (can be replaced with bay leaves, but it's not as authentic!)
— 2 tablespoons of oil (sunflower or coconut)
— juice of half a lime
— salt — to taste

3. **Preparing the rice base — the white sail of the dish.**

Take the already cooked rice — it should be as crumbly as sand on a tropical beach. It's best to use rice that has been in the fridge — it won't stick in the pan. Ready? Then forward to the spicy raid!

4. **Pirate explosion: frying the spices!**

Ask an adult to place the pan on medium heat and add oil. When it heats up, add the mustard seeds. Oh! They will start to jump like rascals on a ship. Don't be scared — it's normal! Quickly add the curry leaves and peanuts — they will be crunchy and tasty.

5. **The golden color of the captain's flag — adding turmeric!**

Add a teaspoon of turmeric to the spices — it will make the rice sun-yellow. Stir everything carefully with a wooden spatula. Smell it? The spirit of Malabar has awakened!

6. **Time for rice — the main part of the adventure!**

Add the cooked rice to the pan. Stir slowly so that the spices cover each grain of rice. Don't rush — a true pirate knows that even rice wants to be spoken to gently!

7. **Lime juice — a breeze of ocean freshness.**

Squeeze the juice of half a lime directly into the pan. It will make the dish fresh and slightly sour, like the sea breeze at dawn. Add a little salt — and your lemon rice is ready to look like a dish from a pirate palace!

8. **Serving — how to present a dish of captain's rank.**

Place the rice in a deep plate. Garnish with a few curry leaves or a slice of lime. Want to make it even more impressive? Add some toasted coconut or crunchy mustard seeds on top!

9. **Secrets from the galley's hideout.**

— Use crumbly rice — sticky rice won't give that "pirate" effect.
— Mustard seeds burn quickly — fry them for just a few seconds!
— Peanuts can be replaced with cashews or sunflower seeds if you want a new adventure.

10. **Careful, young sailor: spices are hot, like a volcano on the spice island!**

When the spices are frying — don't lean too close. Don't touch the pan without a glove or towel. And don't try the hot dish with a spoon — wait a minute. Even a pirate needs caution!

Your lemon rice is ready, captain!

This is not just a dish — it's a journey of taste! Bright, crunchy, fresh, with the aroma of the Malabar coast, where palms whisper, and spices dance in the pan. Eat slowly, imagining a tropical shore and a pirate camp, where every day begins with a new delicious discovery. Bon voyage, young chef!

Vegetable Stew "Thoran": Pirate Stew from the Rainforest!

1. **Ahoy, young sailor! Today we are cooking pirate vegetable stew — "Thoran"!**

On the Malabar Coast, where spices grow thicker than seaweed in the tropical sea, pirates loved a special dish — *Thoran*. It's a tender, vibrant vegetable stew with coconut, cooked quickly but with love. Are you ready to become the captain of the vegetable ship? Call an adult navigator — and let's set sail on a culinary voyage!

2. **Preparing the treasure map of ingredients.**

Find in the pantry:
— 1 cup finely chopped cabbage
— 1 medium carrot (grated or finely chopped)
— a handful of green beans (can be replaced with string beans)
— 1/2 cup grated coconut
— 1 teaspoon mustard seeds
— 1/2 teaspoon turmeric
— 1 teaspoon garlic-ginger paste (or just garlic)
— 6-8 curry leaves (or bay leaves)
— 2 tablespoons oil
— salt — to taste

3. **Preparing the vegetables — pirate-style chopping!**

Chop the cabbage, carrots, and beans into small pieces — as if searching for treasures in each vegetable! If a knife is too serious a weapon, ask an adult for help. The grated coconut should be soft, like the sand on the shores of Malabar.

4. **Pirate fleet on the stove — frying the spices!**

Heat the oil in a pan. Add the mustard seeds — they will start to jump like pirates during a dance. Quickly add the curry leaves (if available) and the ginger-garlic paste. The aroma is like a signal of culinary victory!

5. **Diving into the waves of vegetables.**

Now add all the cabbage, carrots, and beans to the pan. Sprinkle with turmeric and salt. Stir like a captain steering his crew. Cover with a lid and simmer for 5-7 minutes on medium heat until the vegetables are soft but not falling apart.

6. **Coconut storm — adding sweet snow!**

When the vegetables are almost ready, add the grated coconut. It gives the dish a sweet taste and softness. Stir everything once more — and you'll see the vegetables play as if under a tropical rain.

7. **Final touch — and to the table!**

A few more minutes — and you can take it off the heat. Don't overcook — the vegetables should be colorful, fragrant, like a parrot on an old pirate's shoulder. Done!

8. **Serving — like in the captain's hold!**

Serve Thoran with boiled rice or simply in a bowl garnished with green leaves. If you like — sprinkle a few crunchy nuts or croutons on top. A true Malabar pirate would be delighted!

9. **Culinary secrets from the pirate galley.**

— Use fresh or frozen coconut — it's the tastiest!
— Turmeric gives a yellow color — don't overdo it, or it will be bitter.
— If you want a different option — replace the beans with zucchini or cauliflower.

10. **Careful, young sailor: spices are hot, and oil is not a sea for swimming!**

When adding spices to hot oil — keep your distance, don't get too close with your face! The pan is hot, so use a kitchen spatula and towel. Never leave the fire unattended — even pirates had rules!

That's it, captain! Your "Thoran" is ready for boarding!

This is not just a vegetable stew — it's the music of spices, the whisper of coconut, and a tropical story locked in one pan. Eat slowly, savoring each bite, imagining a tropical shore, palm trees, and a merry band of pirates laughing around the fire. Well done! To new taste adventures!

Koonthal Fry: Spicy Squids from the Pirate's Wharf!

1. **Hello, sea wolf! It's time to fry squids — Koonthal Fry style!**

On the hot shores of Malabar, where the sea roars and spices can be smelled from miles away, pirates prepared a special dish — *Koonthal Fry*. These are fried squids in a spicy marinade with garlic, red pepper, and lime juice. Want to become the main chef on a tropical ship? Then turn on your imagination, call an adult helper, and set sail for a culinary boarding!

2. **Ingredients — treasures from pirate ports.**

Prepare:
— 300 g of squids (cleaned, cut into rings — ask an adult)
— 1 teaspoon of garlic paste
— 1/2 teaspoon of ground red pepper (or sweet paprika for children)
— 1/2 teaspoon of turmeric
— juice of half a lime
— salt — to taste
— 2–3 tablespoons of oil for frying (sunflower or coconut)

3. **Preparing the squids — how to clean without catching an ink stain.**

Cleaning squids is a task for an adult. Once the squids are cleaned and cut into rings, rinse them well under cold water. Then pat them dry with a paper towel — squids don't like to be wet when they go into battle (i.e., the pan).

4. **Marinade — a spicy armor for the squids.**

In a deep bowl, mix: garlic paste, red pepper or paprika, turmeric, lime juice, and salt. Carefully coat all the squid rings in this mixture. Now they should turn golden-red — like the sunset in the Caribbean!

5. **A little rest — marinating with the taste of the sea.**

Leave the squids in the marinade for 10–15 minutes. During this time, the spices will penetrate every cell, and the lime juice will make the meat soft and aromatic — like the adventures remembered by an old bottle with a message.

6. **Frying — a pan that roars like a hold in a storm!**

Heat the pan with oil. Ask an adult to help — hot oil is dangerous! When the oil is warm, carefully place the squid rings. Fry for 2–3 minutes on each side — no more! Squids are very sensitive: if overcooked, they become rubbery, like ropes on a mast.

7. **Color and aroma — a signal to the captain that the dish is ready!**

As soon as the squids are browned and firm, remove them from the heat. Now the kitchen smells like a spice market in the city of Kozhikode. All the sailors are already lining up with their plates!

8. **Serving — how to decorate a pirate feast.**

Place the squids on a plate, sprinkle with fresh herbs or a few drops of lime juice. Serve with rice, chapati flatbreads, or simply in a paper "ship" for a snack. Want more effect? Add thinly sliced onions, fried until crispy!

9. **Galley secrets: how to make it better than in the port.**

— Do not fry the squids longer than necessary — they are quick, like pirates on a boarding.
— You can add a pinch of ground fennel — it will make the aroma deeper.
— If there is no garlic paste — grate a clove of garlic or ask a helper.

10. **Careful, young sailor: the pan is hot, like gunpowder in a cannon!**

Do not touch the hot oil, do not try freshly fried food straight from the fire — wait a minute! And remember: cooking is fun, but with rules, like in every true pirate expedition.

Your Koonthal Fry is ready, captain!

This is not just a dish — it's an explosion of the sea, spices, and bravery. Fried squids were respected even on flagship ships! So grab a spoon, call the crew — and enjoy a delicious voyage into new culinary adventures!

Lassi with Cumin and Salt: Coolness for the True Pirates of Malabar!

1. Ahoy, young captain! Want to cool down after spices and sun?

When the Malabar pirates returned from their hot journeys to the spice islands, they didn't drink lemonade or tap water. They made *salty lassi with cumin* — a refreshing yogurt drink that washes away fatigue like a wave washes away sand. Today, you will learn to make this magical elixir — but don't forget to call the first mate to ensure everything is safe and fun!

2. Treasures in the hold — ingredients for Malabar coolness.

Prepare:
— 1 cup of natural yogurt (unsweetened)
— 1/2 cup of cold water
— 1/4 teaspoon of ground cumin
— a pinch of salt (sea salt, like real pirates, if you wish!)
— ice cubes (optional)

Got everything? Then let's set sail to the culinary port — to whip up some lassi!

3. Yogurt — like waves on the tops of a coral reef.

Pour the yogurt into a jug or deep bowl. It should be thick, like fog at dawn in the harbor. If it's too thick, add a little water and stir well with a spoon or whisk. You can imagine it's the wheel of your ship, cutting through the waves!

4. Adding water — the sea to the yogurt boat.

Add half a cup of cold water (from the fridge, if you like). Stir everything until the drink becomes uniform and slightly frothy. This transforms your drink into a real *lassi* — frothy, cool, and pleasant for every sailor.

5. Cumin — the secret spice from a tropical island.

Cumin is not just a seasoning. It's the ship's treasure of flavor! Take a pinch of ground cumin and add it to the drink. Even better — toast the cumin a bit on a dry pan (only with an adult!) and then crush it — the aroma will be like from a spice chest in Kerala!

6. Salt — the pirate's zest!

Add a pinch of salt. You can imagine it's the crumbs of sea foam that add flavor. Don't overdo it — one pinch works wonders, two — a storm on the ship :)

7. Mixing — the true captain's shaker.

Now beat everything well — with a spoon, whisk, or (if you have one) a small blender. The drink should be silky and frothy. If you like, throw in a few ice cubes. Oh, now your glass looks like the sea under the moon!

8. Serving — how to serve a drink from a tropical tavern.

Pour into clear glasses or clay mugs — real Malabar pirates loved clay cups because they keep cool longer. Garnish on top with a pinch of cumin or a mint leaf if you want to add a touch of green!

9. Secrets of Malabar coolness.

— Lassi is tastiest when very cold. So use chilled water or even store it in the fridge a bit before serving.
— Cumin can be combined with a pinch of crushed ginger — this will make the drink even more vibrant.
— Instead of salt, you can add a pinch of black salt (Indian) if you want pirate authenticity.

10. Careful, young sailor: don't get carried away with the blender without permission!

Blenders, whisks, and sharp spices are tools for a responsible cook. So start all electrical devices only with an adult! And don't drink lassi straight from the blender — pour it into a glass like a true deck officer.

Your salty lassi with cumin is ready, captain of coolness!

This is not just a drink — it's a breath of tropical wind that refreshes and energizes. Pirates drink it when they return from spicy lunches or hot adventures. Made lassi — you're not just a cook, you're a sea alchemist! To new tasty journeys, my young friend!

Unniyappam: Sweet Balls of Happiness from Bananas and Coconut!

1. Hey, sweet sailor! It's time to make unniyappam — a dessert that tastes like treasure!

When the Malabar pirates celebrated their victories, they fried *unniyappam* — small sweet pancake balls made from rice flour, ripe bananas, coconut, and spices. They are crispy on the outside, soft on the inside, and smell like the sea and celebration! So grab a banana instead of a saber, call an adult navigator, and let's make these delicious pearls together!

2. Gathering ingredients — sweet treasures of the tropics.

Prepare:
— 1 cup of rice flour
— 2 ripe bananas (the softer, the better!)
— 1/2 cup of coconut flakes (or freshly grated coconut)
— 1/4 cup of sugar (or a bit more if you like it sweet)
— 1/4 teaspoon of ground cardamom
— 1/2 teaspoon of baking powder (optional)
— 1/4 cup of water (or coconut milk)
— oil for frying (sunflower or coconut)

3. Banana base — the soft heart of unniyappams.

Peel the bananas and mash them well with a fork or spoon in a deep bowl. It should turn into a puree — thick and fragrant. If you imagine it's a potion of joy, you won't be wrong!

4. **Mixing ingredients — the magic begins!**

Add coconut, sugar, cardamom, and rice flour to the banana puree. Carefully pour in water or coconut milk — little by little, until the batter is like thick cream. If it's too runny, add a bit more flour. Mix everything — you should have a fragrant, sweet mixture.

5. **Rest before the adventure — let the batter sit.**

Let the batter sit for 15–20 minutes. During this time, the flour will absorb moisture, the aromas will blend, and the batter will be ready for frying. You can imagine it's time for a pirate parade on the deck!

6. **Frying — the pan, like a tropical volcanic lagoon.**

Ask an adult to heat some oil in a small deep saucepan. Carefully pour portions of the batter with a spoon (or small ladle) — one ball at a time. They should float in the oil like golden pearls in the sea!

7. **Flip — carefully, so as not to sink!**

When one side turns golden, flip the ball with a fork or slotted spoon. Fry until evenly golden on all sides. This is the real *unniyappam* — sweet, crispy, like a day on the spice shore!

8. **Remove and cool — pirate actions after the storm.**

Place the ready balls on a paper towel — let the oil drain a bit. Then transfer them to a nice plate. Smell that? It's the spirit of the Malabar festival nearby!

9. **Serving — like a dessert for a true captain.**

Serve unniyappam warm or cold. They can be eaten with hands — just like pirates loved! Want to make it even more interesting? Drizzle with a drop of honey or sprinkle with coconut flakes — it will be like tropical snow over a sweet island.

10. **Caution — the main rule of the kitchen deck!**

Hot oil is not a place for exploration! Don't lean too close, don't drop the batter into the oil from a height.

Use a spoon and stay calm. And most importantly — always have an adult nearby!

That's it, young cook-pirate — you've created unniyappam!

This is not just a treat. It's a story from the shores of Kerala, where bananas, coconuts, and cardamom are friends in every dish. Now you know how the festive balls were made by those who traveled the spice routes and loved the sweet life. To new dessert boardings, captain!

Paayasam: Rice Pudding, Sweet as a Treasure!

1. Ahoy, young pirate! Ready to prepare a dessert for the entire ship?

On holidays and after great victories, the Malabar pirates prepared *paayasam* — a delicate, sweet rice pudding cooked in coconut milk, with roasted nuts and raisins. It was a dish for captains! Now it's your time to create this sweet legend. Call your first mate — and let's set sail on a culinary voyage!

2. Gathering ingredients — treasures from the dessert chest.

Prepare:
— 1/4 cup of rice (preferably short-grain)
— 2 cups of water
— 1 cup of coconut milk
— 1/4 cup of sugar (can be a bit more or less)
— 2 tablespoons of cashews
— 2 tablespoons of raisins
— 1/4 teaspoon of cardamom (ground)
— 1 tablespoon of coconut oil or butter (for frying the nuts)

3. We start with rice — the foundation for the sweet ship.

Rinse the rice several times — it should be as clean as the deck after rain. Ask an adult to help with the stove: in a small pot, bring the water to a boil, add the rice, and cook on medium heat for 15–20 minutes until it becomes soft, like a cloud over the ocean. Don't forget to stir!

4. Coconut milk — a wave of tropical tenderness.

When the rice is ready, carefully pour in the coconut milk. Stir. Then add the sugar. Everything cooks for another 5–10 minutes on low heat until the mixture becomes as tender as the mist over Malabar. Don't boil too hard — coconut milk doesn't like turbulent waves!

5. Cardamom — the spice of the pirate festival.

Add a pinch of ground cardamom — it will give the paayasam a magical aroma. You can hold the spice in your palm, smell it — it smells like a tale of distant shores!

6. Frying nuts and raisins — a crunchy surprise in every spoonful.

In a small pan, heat a spoonful of coconut oil or butter. Carefully add the cashews — fry until golden. Then toss in the raisins — they will "puff up" like sails! Do all this with an adult! Hot oil is no place for sweet fingers.

7. Adding the crunchy cargo to the sweet sea.

Add the fried cashews and raisins to the pot with paayasam. Stir gently. Oh, what an aroma! Every pirate in the kitchen is already waiting for their spoon. And you — are the captain of this flavorful ship!

8. Serving — how to present the dessert so everyone says "Wow!"

Paayasam can be served hot or chilled. Pour into a nice bowl, sprinkle a few more nuts or coconut flakes on top. Want a real pirate effect? Garnish with a slice of banana or mint.

9. **Secrets of the Malabar galley.**

— Don't boil coconut milk on high heat — it will turn bitter.
— If you don't have cardamom, replace it with a pinch of vanilla — it will be magical in its own way.
— You can replace cashews with almonds or pistachios — every adventure has its own spices!

10. **Attention, young sailor: hot oil and steam are not for boarding!**

When frying nuts or cooking rice — don't touch the pot, pan, or stove. Use a wooden spoon, a towel, and always be with an adult. Sweets are delightful, but only when safe!

Paayasam is ready, captain of the sweet ocean!

This pudding is like a dessert treasure map: delicate, tropical, with surprises in every spoonful. It's made for holidays, after adventures, and just because — to delight yourself and the crew. Now you know how to create the taste of the Malabar sun in your kitchen. To new dessert discoveries, pirate!

Tiger Prawns in Masala: A Spicy Adventure in Every Tail!

1. **Ahoy, young captain! It's time to cook tiger prawns — like a true pirate from Malabar!**

When fresh tiger prawns washed ashore in Kerala, pirates would throw a spicy feast — frying them in special masala to warm up after sea adventures. Today, you are the ship's cook, and it's up to you to create this aromatic dish! But don't forget to call an adult helmsman — the spices are as hot as midday sand, and the pan doesn't tolerate carelessness!

2. **Ingredients — treasures from the depths of the sea and the spice chest.**

Gather:
— 300 g of tiger prawns (peeled, without shell — ask an adult to help)
— 1 teaspoon of garlic paste
— 1 teaspoon of ginger paste
— 1/2 teaspoon of turmeric
— 1 teaspoon of paprika or sweet chili
— 1/2 teaspoon of ground cumin
— 1/2 teaspoon of coriander (ground)
— juice of half a lime
— salt — to taste
— 2 tablespoons of oil (sunflower or coconut)

3. **Preparing the prawns — not with a saber, but with love!**

The prawns should be well rinsed and dried. Then place them in a bowl, add turmeric, a pinch of salt, and lime juice. This is not only tasty but also helps remove the excess sea smell. Let them marinate while you prepare the masala!

4. **Masala — an aromatic armor for the prawns.**

In a small bowl, mix: ginger and garlic paste, paprika, cumin, coriander, and a pinch of salt. If you imagine it's a magical powder from a spice wizard — you won't be wrong! Add a little water to make a thick paste. This is your *masala*.

5. **The pan is buzzing — time for battle!**

Ask an adult to heat the pan with oil. When it's hot, add the masala and fry for a few seconds, stirring. The aroma will rise like a flag on the ship's mast! Now carefully lay out the prawns — each tail should be covered with masala, like armor against sea monsters.

6. **Fry — but don't overcook!**

Prawns cook very quickly — 2–3 minutes on each side. They should turn pink and slightly browned. Don't cook longer — otherwise, they will become tough, like dry ropes!

7. **The final lime touch.**

Remove the pan from the heat and immediately sprinkle the prawns with lime juice. The aroma will become fresh, like a breeze from the ocean. The Malabar pirates knew: without lime, the dish is like a ship without a compass!

8. **Serving — like a festive dinner on the captain's bridge.**

Serve the prawns with rice or chapati flatbreads. You can garnish with fresh herbs, a slice of lime, or thin rings of red onion. For a true pirate effect — lay the prawns in shells or on a banana leaf!

9. **Secrets of the pirate pan.**

— Marinate the prawns for at least 10 minutes — the spices need time to penetrate inside.
— Add a pinch of sugar to the masala — it will enhance the flavor.
— If you want it less spicy — use more paprika instead of chili.

10. **Careful, young sailor: hot is not a wave, it's a danger!**

Hot oil and pan — this is a zone for a careful helmsman. Don't touch with your hands, don't lean over. Stir with a spatula and always be with an adult. Remember: even the tastiest dish is not worth injuries!

That's it, spice captain! Tiger prawns in masala — ready for boarding!

This is not just fried prawns. This is a Malabar adventure, where spices whisper stories, and each tail is a new taste. Now you are a true cook from the spice coast. To new culinary sails, young pirate!

Fish Curry with Rice: A Pirate Dish with the Deep Aroma of the Ocean!

1. **Yo-ho-ho, Captain! We are preparing the main dish of a pirate's lunch — fish curry with rice!**

On the Malabar coast, where spices grow under palm trees and seagulls sing sea songs, fishermen and pirates cooked *curry with sea fish*. It was, of course, served with fluffy rice that absorbed all the aromas of the sauce. So grab a spoon, call an adult navigator — and let's start the culinary journey!

2. **Ingredients — a true tropical catch.**

For the fish curry:
— 300 g of white fish fillet (boneless)
— 1 onion
— 1 tomato
— 1 clove of garlic
— 1 teaspoon of ginger paste
— 1/2 teaspoon of turmeric
— 1 teaspoon of sweet paprika or mild chili
— 1/2 teaspoon of ground coriander
— 1 cup of coconut milk
— salt — to taste
— 1 tablespoon of oil
— a few curry leaves or a bay leaf

For the rice:
— 1 cup of rice
— 2 cups of water
— a pinch of salt

3. **Cooking the rice — the foundation of the ship's meal.**

Rinse the rice until the water is clear — this will make it fluffy. Ask an adult to put the water on the heat, add salt, and cook the rice covered on low heat for 15-18 minutes. When the grains become soft, remove from heat and leave covered — let it "mature" like a true sailor before boarding.

4. **Preparing the fish — use a spoon of spices instead of a saber.**

Rinse the fish, cut into large pieces. Sprinkle a little turmeric and salt — this will help the fish retain its shape and aroma. Leave for 10 minutes while you prepare the curry base.

5. **Aromatic masala — the heart of the curry, the soul of the pirate flavor.**

Heat oil in a pan. Add chopped onion, then garlic and ginger paste. When everything turns golden, add tomato, coriander, and paprika. Simmer until the mixture turns into a sauce — thick and aromatic, like a tropical night.

6. **Add the fish — and the curry comes to life!**

Place the fish pieces directly into the sauce. Don't stir too much — the fish is as delicate as a seagull's feather. Pour in the coconut milk, add curry leaves (or bay leaf) and a little water if needed. Bring to a gentle simmer and cook for 10 minutes — until soft and full of aromatic magic.

7. **Final touches — like a flag on the ship's mast.**

When the sauce thickens, taste it: is there enough salt, spices, coconut tenderness? If needed, add a little lime juice for freshness. Remove from heat. Your curry is ready to sail on a plate next to the rice island!

8. **Serving — a pirate feast of flavor.**

On a large plate, lay out the rice, and on top — a generous portion of curry with fish and sauce. You can garnish with greens or a few toasted nuts — for a touch of tropical luxury. Don't forget the spoon — but true pirates can eat with their fingers (clean, of course!).

9. **Secrets of the pirate galley.**

— Use fish that is not too soft — it holds better in the sauce.
— Add grated coconut to the masala — it will be even more aromatic!
— If you want a thicker sauce — evaporate more water.
— It's better to add coconut milk at the end, on low heat.

10. **Careful, young sailor: a hot stove and pot are not galley games!**

Never leave the fire unattended. Don't taste the boiling sauce — it's as hot as lava from the spice island! All hot actions — only with an adult nearby. And your main task is to mix, taste, and create delicious legends!

Hooray! Fish curry with rice — ready to be served on the captain's bridge!

This is not just a lunch — it's a full-fledged sea story with the aromas of spices, tropical coconut, and the spirit of true Malabar cuisine. You are the hero of the galley, who tamed fish and spices in one plate. Bon voyage, Captain!

Crab Paste with Chapati: A Pirate Spread with the Taste of the Ocean!

1. **Hello, young sailor! Ready to make a sea paste for a ship's snack?**

After great adventures, the Malabar pirates didn't always want to cook curry. Sometimes they made *crab paste* — tender, aromatic, with tropical spices, and spread it on *chapati* — thin flatbreads resembling pirate maps. Today, you'll make this paste yourself — just don't be afraid of the crab (it's already cooked!) and act like a true chef from the spice coast!

Preparing the Crab Paste

2. **Ingredients — treasures from the depths of the ocean and the spice shore:**
— 200 g of cooked crab meat (can be canned or from sticks)
— 1 clove of garlic
— 1 teaspoon of lemon or lime juice
— 1 tablespoon of mayonnaise or yogurt (for tenderness)
— a pinch of salt
— a pinch of ground cumin or pepper (optional)
— a bit of greens — dill, parsley, or coriander
— a few drops of oil (optional)

3. **Let's start — how to mix crab and spices without losing the treasure.**
Place the crab meat in a deep bowl. If it's in pieces, mash it with a spoon or fork. Add the squeezed lime juice, garlic (finely grated or crushed), salt, and greens. Then add mayonnaise or yogurt. Mix everything — it should turn into a soft, fragrant paste. You can taste it with your finger (just make sure it's clean!) — and say "Arrr, delicious!"

4. **The secret of the pirate aroma.**

Add a pinch of cumin or a drop of mustard seed oil if you want a true Malabar flavor. It's not necessary, but it adds the spirit of the southern coast!

Making Chapati — Pirate Flatbreads from the Hot Plate

5. **Ingredients for Chapati:**
— 1 cup of flour (wheat, preferably whole grain)
— 1/4 cup of water
— a pinch of salt
— 1 teaspoon of oil

6. **Kneading the dough — pirate sand turns into bread.**

Mix the flour, salt, and water in a bowl. You can imagine it's a treasure map coming to life! Knead the dough with your hands or a spoon until it becomes soft and elastic. Let it "rest" under a towel for 10 minutes — even dough needs a break after the journey.

7. **Rolling and frying — like a pirate scroll.**

Divide the dough into 4 parts, roll each into a thin circle. Ask an adult to heat the pan (without oil!) and fry for 30–40 seconds on each side until spots appear — like spots on a treasure chest!

Assembling the Dish — and Serving Like True Pirates!

8. **Spreading — don't skimp on the paste!**

Spread the crab paste on the ready chapati, roll it up or fold it in half like a pirate scroll. You can add a slice of cucumber or a lettuce leaf — and it will be a real tropical sandwich.

9. **Secrets of Malabar Presentation:**

— Serve with lime on the side — a bit of juice on top will make the taste brighter.
— Want it spicier? Add a pinch of ground pepper to the paste.
— Instead of chapati, you can use toast if you're short on time.

10. **Be careful, young sailor!**

Garlic and knife — this is the responsibility zone of an adult. Frying chapati on the pan should also be done by the senior helmsman. And you — are the main mixer, taster, and culinary wizard! Always wash your hands before and after cooking, and never touch the hot pan.

Crab paste with chapati is ready, captain!

This is not just a snack — it's the taste of adventure that sails with you! Soft crab filling, crispy chapati, and a bit of spices — that's what real Malabar pirates loved after a storm. So enjoy, tell stories, and get ready for new culinary boardings!

Salty Fish Pancakes "Dosa": Pirate Sails with the Taste of the Ocean!

1. **Hello, young pirate! Today we're making dosa — pancakes that even sharks loved!**

In Malabar, pirates adored *dosa* — large thin pancakes made from fermented batter. And if you add a fish filling to them, you'll get a real dish of a sea hero! Today we will make *salty fish dosas*, just like on a real spice ship. So turn on your imagination, grab a spoon, and call an adult helmsman — culinary sailing ahead!

2. **Ingredients for the batter — like assembling a ship before the storm:**

– 1 cup of rice (regular white) – 1/4 cup of urad dal (yellow lentils) or can be replaced with semolina – 1/4 teaspoon of salt – water for soaking and mixing

3. **Preparing the batter — pirate alchemy of time.**

Rinse the rice and urad dal, soak them in water for 4–6 hours (or better — overnight). Then (with the help of an adult) grind everything in a blender with a small amount of water — the batter should not be too liquid but flowing like a sea wave. Add salt and leave for another 6–8 hours (or overnight) in a warm place — the batter should slightly ferment. This is the secret to fluffy dosa!

4. **Treasures for the filling:**

– 200 g of white fish fillet (e.g., tilapia or dorado) – 1 small onion – 1 clove of garlic – 1/2 teaspoon of turmeric – salt — to taste – 1/2 teaspoon of paprika – 1 tablespoon of oil – lime juice (optional)

5. **Cooking the fish — like catching it in the pan.**

Ask an adult to help sauté the chopped onion and garlic in a pan with oil. Add the fish cut into pieces, sprinkle with salt, turmeric, and paprika. Fry for 5–7 minutes until done, stirring constantly, until the fish falls apart into tender pieces. Optionally, add a drop of lime juice. The filling is like a golden treasure!

6. **Baking the dosa — sails on the culinary deck.**

Ask an adult to heat the pan. Pour a little oil. Pour 1 ladle of batter in the center of the pan and carefully spread it in circular motions — like a pirate unfolding a treasure map! Fry for 2–3 minutes until the bottom becomes golden. Place some fish filling on top, fold the dosa in half or roll it up.

7. **Cooking more — the crew is waiting for their portion!**

Continue making dosas with filling for the entire pirate crew. They can be kept warm in foil or served immediately — with yogurt, greens, or sauce.

8. **Pirate tips for perfect pancakes:**

– The batter should be liquid like creamy rain — not thick and not watery. – Before each new dosa, grease the pan with a drop of oil. – Want to make the dosa crispier? Add 1 teaspoon of semolina to the batter. – The fish can be replaced with boiled potatoes or vegetables if you want a different raid.

9. **Caution — the main rule on the kitchen ship!**

A hot pan and heated batter can cause a storm! Do not touch the pan with your hands, do not flip the pancakes without a spatula. Always ask for adult help when frying and turning on the stove. Cook with attention, and serve with a pirate sparkle in your eyes!

That's it, captain! Your fish dosa is ready to be served on the helmsman's table!

This is not just a pancake — it's a crispy pirate sail filled with the aromas of the ocean and spices. Eat slowly, dream of distant shores and new tastes — and get ready for the next culinary voyage!

Pirates of the South China Sea

1. **Breakfast in the Bay: Rice Rolls and Dried Fish.**

Pirates of the South China Sea — from the regions of Vietnam, southern China, Taiwan, and the Philippines — started their day with a delicious yet convenient breakfast. A popular dish was steamed rice rolls "cheung fun" or "banh cuon" filled with shrimp, mushrooms, or vegetables. They were often served with thinly sliced dried or smoked fish, providing strength before heading out to sea. The drink — warm jasmine tea or rice broth with pieces of ginger.

2. **Fish Soup "Tom Yum with Shrimp": Sour-Spicy Energy.**

For lunch, pirates prepared the sour-spicy soup "tom yum" with shrimp or fish, which became a true legend of the coast. The broth included lemongrass, galangal, kaffir lime leaves, chili, fish sauce, and a bit of lime juice. This soup not only warmed but also cleared the mind after a storm. It was served with boiled rice or noodles, and often simply drunk from cups — right on the deck!

3. **Main Course: Fried Fish with Soy Sauce and Ginger.**

For dinner, pirates enjoyed fried sea fish (often barramundi, mackerel, or grouper) cooked with ginger, garlic, green onions, and soy sauce. The fish was fried to a crispy crust, but inside it remained juicy. It was served with rice, and sometimes with a vegetable sauce based on eggplants or bamboo shoots. The dish was simple but filled with depth of flavor.

4. **Side Dishes: Sticky Rice and Fermented Vegetables.**

A favorite side dish was aromatic sticky rice cooked in coconut milk or with the addition of garlic. Sour, slightly salty vegetables — fermented cabbage, daikon, or carrots — were often served. These vegetables were prepared in advance, stored in jars right on the ship, and they lasted a long time, which was very convenient for pirate journeys.

5. **Pirate Snack: Shrimp Crackers and Fried Octopus.**

When craving a crunchy snack, pirates fried shrimp chips or prepared "tod man kung" — small cakes made from minced shrimp with herbs and spices. They were fried in a large pan and served with a sweet and sour sauce. Also popular were pieces of octopus marinated in ginger and fried to a golden crust — a true sea delicacy.

6. **Beverages: Lotus Tea and Sweet Coconut Infusion.**

In the tropical climate, pirates drank a lot of fluids. The most popular was tea made from lotus petals or roasted rice — light, refreshing, aromatic. Also, a coconut infusion with palm sugar, which was drunk chilled. This drink restored strength after a hard day, provided calm, and was very popular among the younger crew members.

7. **Desserts from the Sea and Sushi: Rice Balls and Seaweed Jelly.**

For dessert, pirates prepared rice balls filled with bean paste or coconut sugar — "buchi" or "mochi". Sometimes they served agar-agar jelly — seaweed, with the addition of mango or lychee. These desserts were light, sweet, and chilled — the perfect end to a hot day among sails and waves.

8. **Communal Dinner on the Boat — A Ritual of Unity.**

When the ship was anchored, the crew gathered together for a communal meal. Everyone brought their dish or ingredient: someone caught fish, someone cut vegetables, others cooked rice. The dishes were placed on banana leaves, eaten with hands or chopsticks. It was not just a meal — it was a tradition of unity, where each dish had a story, and each dinner — its own song.

9. **Provisions for Sailing: Dried Fish, Shrimp, and Rice Cakes.**

For long sea voyages, pirates stored dried fish and shrimp, which were wrapped in rice paper and dried in the sun. They also prepared rice cakes with meat or vegetables, stored in bamboo boxes. Such dishes did not spoil for several days and were ideal for eating during sailing or on stormy days when it was impossible to cook hot meals.

10. **Cuisine of the South China Sea — A Journey of Flavors and Cultures.**

The cuisine of the pirates of the South China Sea is a true melting pot of cultures: Chinese, Vietnamese, Filipino, Thai. It features sweet and sour flavors, crunchy snacks, spicy soups, and delicate desserts. It teaches not only how to cook but also to appreciate diversity, share, and create new even in the most turbulent seas.

The pirate cuisine of the South China Sea is a true treasure of aromas and traditions. It offers the taste of adventure, showing how a whole world can be hidden in simple ingredients. And most importantly — it teaches that shared food unites better than any anchor. So — ready for new culinary raids?

Fish Soup Tom Yum: A Fiery Dish from the South China Sea!

1. **Signal for a culinary raid, young captain!**

The pirates of the South China Sea knew: a true fighter is not afraid of a spicy taste! Today we will prepare Tom Yum fish soup — hot, aromatic, and spicy, just like the adventures themselves! But remember: spicy food requires caution. Call the first mate (mom, dad, or grandma), put on a kitchen apron, and set off on a culinary hunt!

2. **Treasures from the market: ingredients for the soup.**

Here's a list of what to look for in the holds:
— 200 g of white fish fillet (can be sea or river)
— 1 liter of water or fish broth
— 1 stalk of lemongrass (or lemon zest if unavailable)
— 2-3 kaffir lime leaves (can be replaced with lime zest)
— 1 small chili pepper (or a bit of paprika without heat)
— 2-3 champignons or other mushrooms
— 2 tablespoons of lime juice
— 1 tablespoon of fish sauce or salt
— 1 teaspoon of sugar
— a few leaves of cilantro or parsley

3. **Preparation — like a pirate attack plan!**

Cut the fish into small pieces. Slice the mushrooms. If you have lemongrass or lime leaves — wash and slightly crush them with a spoon to release the aroma. And chili — be careful! Ask an adult to cut it, as it's as fiery as a hot ship's cannon!

4. **Launch the cauldron on the water — let's start cooking!**

Pour water or broth into a pot and put it on the fire. Add lemongrass, lime leaves, and chili pepper. Let it boil for 5 minutes so the aroma penetrates every drop! The smell will be tropical — like a storm of spices is approaching!

5. Time for the fish — the main chest of flavor.

Add the fish pieces to the broth. Cook for 5-7 minutes — no more! Fish is delicate and doesn't like to be cooked for long. During this time, add the mushrooms. They will add mystery to the soup, like sea caves with pearls.

6. Pirate spices — a balance of fire and sweetness.

Add fish sauce (or a bit of salt), lime juice, and sugar. This is the magical trio of Thai cuisine: sour, salty, sweet. This is how pirates cooked under the scorching sun to regain strength after a storm!

7. The secret trick of kitchen pirates.

If the soup is too spicy, add a bit of coconut milk or a spoonful of yogurt — it will calm the flame. Pirates learned to cook with what was at hand — they were true wizards in the cauldron!

8. The finishing touch — like a flag on the mast.

Remove the soup from the heat and let it stand for 5 minutes. Then place cilantro or parsley leaves on top. The aroma will be such that even seagulls will come for lunch!

9. Serve the soup as a pirate treasure.

Pour Tom Yum into a deep plate. It can be served with rice or rice noodles. If you want — add a piece of lime on the side so everyone can add some tanginess to taste. Pirates loved freedom — even on a plate!

10. Warning from Admiral Cambuzia.

— Do not touch your eyes after handling the pepper — wash your hands!
— You control the spiciness — it's not necessary to add a lot of chili.
— Always work with an adult nearby — especially when cooking or cutting.
— And don't forget: the main spice is a good mood!

Here it is — fish Tom Yum, spicy and aromatic, like adventures under the sails!

This soup came to us from the shores of Thailand and the South China Sea, where sailors knew the taste. You have prepared not just a dish, but a whole story — a story of pirates, spices, and ocean treasures. Bon appétit, little captain! The next journey is already beyond the horizon!

Shrimps in Sweet and Sour Sauce: A Sea Adventure in Every Spoon!

1. Yo-ho-ho, little kitchen pirate, it's time to cook some deliciousness!

Today, we are preparing a dish loved by all the pirates of the Gulf of Siam — shrimps in sweet and sour sauce! It could be found in every port of the South China Sea because it's simple, tasty, and smells like the tropics. Jump into the galley, but don't forget: here, like on the deck, you need attention and an adult helper!

2. Treasure map — ingredients for our adventure:

Prepare your basket and search for:
— 200 g of peeled shrimps (medium or large)
— 2 tablespoons of ketchup
— 1 tablespoon of soy sauce
— 1 teaspoon of sugar
— 2-3 tablespoons of pineapple juice (or orange juice)
— 1 tablespoon of vinegar (apple or rice)
— 1 teaspoon of cornstarch + 2 tablespoons of water
— 1 clove of garlic
— a bit of vegetable oil
— a few pieces of pineapple or pepper for brightness

3. **Preparing the shrimps — without a harpoon and with respect!**

The shrimps should already be cleaned. If not, ask an adult to help remove the shell and the "string" from the back (that's the vein). Rinse the shrimps with cold water and pat dry. They should be fresh and shiny — as if just caught from the net!

4. **Preparing the magical sweet and sour sauce — with a hint of a tropical storm!**

In a bowl, mix: ketchup, soy sauce, pineapple juice, vinegar, and sugar. This is the secret recipe from the stash of Chinese pirates! Mix well with a spoon. Separately, dissolve the cornstarch in two tablespoons of water — it will make the sauce thick and shiny, like a treasure at the bottom of the sea!

5. **The galley is battle-ready — let's start frying!**

Pour a little oil into the pan and heat it up (an adult will do this!). Add the chopped garlic — the smell will be so enticing that even the parrot on the mast will get hungry. After a few seconds, add the shrimps. Fry for 2–3 minutes until they turn pink. Don't overcook — they are as delicate as coral shells!

6. **The adventure continues — add the sauce to the shrimps.**

Pour the sweet and sour sauce into the pan. Stir and watch as it thickens. Then add the cornstarch with water. The sauce will envelop the shrimps like a storm envelops a ship — aroma and shine in every drop!

7. **Add colors — pineapple, pepper, and imagination.**

Throw pieces of pineapple or red sweet pepper into the pan. They will add brightness and a tropical mood. Pirates loved food that was not only tasty but also looked like treasures!

8. **Serving — a pirate feast on every plate!**

Place the shrimps on a plate. You can serve a bit of rice alongside — it absorbs the sauce wonderfully. Garnish with greens or a slice of lime. Want more effect? Serve everything on a large lettuce leaf — like on an island from pirate legends!

9. **Secrets of the pirate chef:**

— Shrimps should be cooked quickly — then they are juicy.
— If there's no pineapple, you can use mandarin or orange.
— Want a lighter dish? Use less oil and more vegetables.
— Everything can be cooked without hot pepper — it's not necessary.

10. **Warning from the kitchen captain:**

— A hot pan is not a toy!
— Don't taste raw shrimps! They should be completely pink.
— After work, wash your hands, especially if you handled garlic or vinegar.
— And don't forget the main rule of pirate cooking: cook with a smile and a taste for adventure!

That's it — the dish is ready!

Shrimps in sweet and sour sauce are like a fun storm from the South China Sea: bright, tasty, and a little unexpected. You just repeated a recipe enjoyed by captains and cooks at the sea markets of Siam. Now your kitchen has become part of the pirate map of flavors.

Steamed Fish with Ginger: A Light Dish for True Sea Captains!

1. **Young captain, it's time to set sail on a culinary voyage!**

Today we have a very special dish — steamed fish with ginger. This is food for wise pirates who want to be agile, strong, and healthy like sea dragons! It's easy to prepare, but it's important to be attentive and work together with an adult. Put on your apron, call your helper — and to the galley!

2. **Pirate's map of ingredients — searching for tropical treasures:**

Here's what you need to find:
— 2 fillets of white fish (e.g., sea bass or tilapia)
— A piece of fresh ginger (3-4 cm)
— 1 clove of garlic
— 1 tablespoon of soy sauce
— A bit of green onion or cilantro
— A few drops of lemon or lime juice
— A pinch of salt
— A steamer or a colander + a pot with a lid

3. **Prepare the fish — like preparing sails before a storm.**

The fish needs to be rinsed under cold water and dried. If there are bones — ask an adult to remove them. Then lightly salt the fillets to fully reveal the taste of the sea. Pirates loved this dish in the ports of China — it's light and very aromatic!

4. **Slice the ginger — the secret root of the East!**

Peel the ginger with a knife or a spoon (it scrapes easily). Slice it into thin slices or strips. Do the same with the garlic. Remember: ginger is not just a spice, but a true guardian against colds! Its scent is as fresh as the sea breeze at dawn.

5. **Gather everything together — preparing for the steam.**

Place the fish on a plate suitable for steaming. Top it with ginger and garlic, drizzle with soy sauce. You can add a bit of lemon juice. Does it look beautiful? The aroma is even better!

6. **The captain's steam boiler — how to create a steamer.**

If you have a steamer — great! If not, we'll make a pirate version: pour a little water into a pot (2-3 cm), place a colander or rack inside. On it — the plate with the fish. Cover with a lid, like treasure in a chest. Ask an adult to put everything on the fire.

7. **The steam works — like smoke from ship cannons.**

Steam is hot, so don't open the lid yourself! Let the fish cook for 10–15 minutes (depending on the thickness of the pieces). Its meat will become white, soft, and easily separated with a fork. This is the true magic of the East!

8. **Decorate like a pirate map — greens and sauce.**

Sprinkle with green onion or cilantro on top. You can add a bit more soy sauce. Want some brightness? Add a piece of red pepper (not hot!) — like a compass on the plate. Such fish would be the highlight of any feast in a pirate port!

9. **Secrets of wise Asian chefs:**

— Ginger can be replaced with lemon zest if it's not available.
— If you're afraid of a strong taste — use less garlic.
— It's better not to overcook the fish — it will become dry.
— If you have a banana leaf — you can wrap the fillet in it for beauty!

10. **Warnings from the senior galley:**

— Steam is very hot! Always ask an adult to open the lid.
— Don't touch the metal parts of the steamer — they will burn.
— Don't forget to wash your hands after working with fish.
— And most importantly — cook with the heart and curiosity of a true sailor!

Here it is — tender steamed fish with the aroma of ginger and the breath of the sea breeze!

This dish was prepared by wise fishermen and pirates of the South China Sea when they wanted to truly relax after a storm. It's light but full of flavor and energy. Now you know the secrets of steam magic — so get ready for new culinary adventures!

Fried Rice with Squid: A Treasure Chest of Flavor from the Depths of the South China Sea!

1. Ahoy, young pirate! The galley awaits — let's prepare a treasure from the sea!

Today we will learn how to cook fried rice with squid — a favorite dish of pirates and fishermen of the South China Sea! This is an aromatic, hearty, and very fun dish for true kitchen captains. The main thing is attention, adult assistance, and a spirit of adventure!

2. Ingredient map — searching for sea treasures and rice gold:

Find in the holds:
— 1 cup of cooked rice (preferably from yesterday, cooled)
— 150–200 g of squid (fresh or frozen)
— 1 egg
— 1 carrot
— ½ onion or green onion
— 1 clove of garlic
— 1 tablespoon of soy sauce
— a little oil for frying
— a pinch of salt and pepper

3. Squid — sea acrobats on your frying pan!

If the squid is raw, ask an adult to help clean it: remove the skin, extract the "backbone" (transparent plate), and cut the squid into rings. If they are already cut, just defrost and rinse. Squid should be cooked carefully — like the inhabitants of the depths, they are tender and cook quickly!

4. Chopping treasures: vegetables to battle!

Cut the carrot into strips or small cubes. Chop the onion finely. Grate or crush the garlic. These ingredients will give our rice not only taste but also color — like flags from different islands!

5. Heat the pan — like a battle cannon on a ship!

Ask an adult to help with the stove. Pour a little oil and add the garlic. Fry for a few seconds until a spicy aroma appears. Then add the squid and fry for 1–2 minutes, no more! They should become white and slightly firm. Remove them from the pan — they will return later!

6. Egg — the binder of the entire fleet!

In the same pan, crack the egg. Quickly stir it with a spoon or spatula to form soft pieces. This is like foam on the waves, tasty and healthy. The egg will make the rice more tender and nutritious.

7. Time for rice — the golden cargo has arrived!

Add the cooked rice to the pan. If it is clumped, break it up with a spoon. Pirates always used yesterday's rice — it doesn't turn into mush and fries well. Mix everything thoroughly!

8. Return the squid to the bay!

Add the squid back to the pan. Then add the carrot and onion. Drizzle with soy sauce and add a little salt and pepper. Mix everything together. All the ingredients should dance together like a crew on deck before a storm!

9. Secrets from the kitchen navigators:

— Do not fry the squid for long — they will become rubbery.
— You can add green peas, corn, or pineapple — it will be more fun!
— If the rice is too soft, spread it on a plate and cool it before frying.
— Want color? Use egg yolk, red pepper, or curry!

10. Warning from Captain Cambuzia:

— A hot pan is not a beach, it's hot! Do not touch it without adult help.
— Be careful with raw eggs — wash your hands after handling them.
— Do not leave the dish while frying — it cooks quickly.
— And most importantly: the captain does not leave his crew — fry together with a helper!

Done! Fried rice with squid — a true sea treasure!

This dish was eaten by pirates in the port cities of Malaysia, Vietnam, and Thailand — where spices meet seafood. Now in your plate — the warm taste of the Far East, tropics, and the sea. Bon appétit, young captain! The next dish is already on the horizon!

Chinese Dumplings with Shrimp: Delicious Sailboats from the East!

1. Ahoy, young culinary corsair! It's time to prepare edible boats — dumplings!

Chinese dumplings with shrimp are a beloved treasure of the South China Sea's kitchens. They were made not only in cities but also on the decks of pirate junks! On the outside — delicate dough, inside — treasures from the sea. Put on your apron, call an adult navigator, and let's prepare these treats together!

2. Ingredient list — a culinary treasure map:

For the dough:
— 2 cups of wheat flour
— ¾ cup of hot water (not boiling!)
— a pinch of salt

For the filling:
— 200 g of peeled shrimp
— 1 small carrot
— 2 leaves of Chinese cabbage (can be substituted with white cabbage)
— 1 clove of garlic
— 1 tsp of soy sauce
— a pinch of sugar and salt
— a drop of sesame oil (if available)

3. **Kneading the dough — like sewing a ship's sail!**

Mix the flour with salt in a bowl. Slowly pour in the hot water and mix with a spoon (better with an adult). When the dough becomes warm and smooth, knead it with your hands. Wrap it in a towel and let it rest for 20 minutes — let it "rest" before the journey!

4. **Preparing the filling — like gathering treasures on an island!**

Chop the shrimp finely, grate the carrot on a fine grater, and slice the cabbage very thinly. Mix everything in a bowl with soy sauce, a pinch of salt, sugar, garlic, and a drop of sesame oil. The filling should be fragrant, like the wind over a bay of spices!

5. **Rolling out the dough — creating the hulls of future ships!**

Divide the dough into small balls (the size of a pirate coin!). Roll each ball into a thin circle. The dumpling skin should be thin but strong — like a sail in a storm!

6. **Shaping the dumplings — like assembling a fleet in the bay!**

Place a little filling in the center of each circle. Fold the dough in half and seal the edges by pinching with your fingers. You can make a wavy edge — it looks like waves on the sea. If the edges don't stick, moisten your finger with water and apply.

7. **Steaming — like in a real tropical mist!**

Place the dumplings in a steamer (or a colander over a pot of water), lined with cabbage leaves or parchment. Steam for 10–12 minutes. The dumplings will become transparent, and the shrimp inside will turn pink, like corals!

8. **Serve like at a pirate feast in Hong Kong!**

Arrange the dumplings on a large platter, like a fleet in formation. Serve with soy sauce or a sauce made of lime, honey, and a drop of vinegar. You can also sprinkle with herbs. Pirates loved to eat dumplings with their hands — straight into adventures!

9. **Secrets of culinary navigators:**

— The filling can be made with fish, chicken, or vegetables if there are no shrimp.
— If the dough tears, add a little flour when rolling out.
— Shaping is fun! You can make different shapes: crescent, boat, shell.
— Want colorful dumplings? Add a little beet juice or carrot juice to the dough!

10. **Warning from Captain Doughsaurus:**

— Hot steam burns — don't open the lid yourself!
— Raw dough is not for eating!
— Use a knife and grater only with an adult helper.
— After shaping, wash your hands and prepare napkins for soy sauce.

Done! Chinese dumplings with shrimp — your culinary fleet to the Eastern shores!

Dumplings are not just food. They are part of an ancient culture that travels the world with chefs, pirates, and travelers. Now you have become the captain of a steamship with the taste of the sea. Bon appétit, brave cook! And don't forget — a true pirate always leaves room for dessert!

Crispy Crab Meat Rolls: Pirate Treasure Wraps!

1. Yo-ho-ho, young kitchen captain, let's prepare to wrap the taste!

Today in the galley — a special task! We will make crispy crab meat rolls — little wraps that hide treasures from the sea. They were prepared by chefs in the ports of Vietnam, Thailand, and Malaysia, and pirates enjoyed them before setting sail. Put on your apron, call an adult helper — and let's navigate to deliciousness!

2. Ingredients — the map to the crispy treasure:

Find in the culinary holds:
— 150 g of crab meat (or crab sticks)
— ½ carrot
— 2 leaves of Chinese or Napa cabbage
— 1 small egg
— 2 tablespoons of mayonnaise or cream cheese
— 5-6 sheets of rice paper or thin spring roll wrappers
— Vegetable oil for frying
— A pinch of salt and pepper
— A bit of green onion or cilantro (optional)

3. Preparing the filling — like gathering treasures at the bottom of the lagoon!

Grate the carrot, chop the cabbage very finely, and mince the crab meat with a knife. Mix everything in a bowl, add the egg, mayonnaise (or cheese), salt, pepper, and greens. Mix until smooth. The filling should be tender but hold together — like a crew on a ship!

4. Preparing the "sails" — sheets for wrapping the rolls.

If using rice paper — soak each sheet in warm water for 10–15 seconds until it becomes soft. If these are ready-made spring roll wrappers — they often don't need soaking. Working with them is like handling sails: gently and carefully!

5. Rolling the rolls — like pirate treasure wraps!

Place a sheet on a board. In the center — a spoonful of filling. Fold the bottom edge to the center, then the sides, and roll into a cylinder. Tightly but carefully — so the filling doesn't escape overboard! The roll should look like a scroll with a secret message.

6. Frying — launching the cannons of taste!

Ask an adult to heat a pan with vegetable oil. Place the rolls seam side down and fry on medium heat for 2–3 minutes on each side until they become golden and crispy, like a real pirate's armor!

7. **Serve as a pirate treat at the post-boarding feast!**

Arrange the ready rolls on a plate, garnish with greens, and place a sauce nearby (soy, sweet and sour, or honey mustard). You can eat them with your hands — just like real sea wolves did!

8. **Secrets of pirate galley wisdom:**

— You can add rice, boiled egg, or cucumber to the filling.
— To prevent the rolls from unrolling — brush the edge with water before frying.
— Don't put too much filling — it makes rolling easier.
— If you don't have rice paper — you can use thin lavash dough or dumpling dough.

9. **Warnings from the senior culinary helmsman:**

— Don't touch the pan yourself — entrust frying to an adult.
— Hot oil is no place for fingers!
— After working with eggs and crabs — be sure to wash your hands.
— Make sure the rolls don't burn — watch them like stars in the sky!

10. **Cook with pleasure — like a real pirate with a kitchen saber!**

The most important thing in pirate cooking is the joy of cooking. In each roll — not only delicious ingredients but also a piece of your imagination, skill, and adventurous spirit!

Done! Crispy crab meat rolls — now your plate is a real sea port of taste!

These wraps were eaten not only in sushi bars but also on ships under the red flag. Now you can prepare a small dish with a big history.

Bon appétit, young culinary corsair! To new taste raids!

Mussel and Nori Soup: A Magical Broth for the Pirates of the Eastern Sea!

1. Ahoy, young captain! Today in the galley — a magical soup!

The pirates of the South China Sea knew: to have the strength of the waves and the wisdom of the sea dragon, one must eat soup made from sea treasures. Today we will prepare a soup with mussels and sea nori — light, aromatic, and very maritime! Call an adult helmsman, put on an apron, and let's prepare the magical broth together!

2. Ingredients — the map to the sea soup:

Find:
— 300 g of mussels (can be in shells or already cleaned)
— 1-1.5 liters of water
— 1 sheet of nori (or 2 small ones)
— 1 tablespoon of soy sauce
— ½ teaspoon of sesame oil (optional)
— 1 small clove of garlic
— a few strips of carrot
— a bit of green onion or parsley
— a pinch of salt and pepper

3. Preparing the mussels — treasures in shells!

If the mussels are in shells — they need to be washed well. Ask an adult to help: the shells need to be cleaned with a brush, and those that are not closed should be discarded. If already cleaned — just rinse with water. Mussels are like jewels in shells, prepare them carefully!

4. Preparing the vegetables — colors of the sea map!

Cut the carrot into thin strips or circles, garlic — very finely. Chop the greens later, before serving. Carrots will add color and a sweet tint to the soup — like a sunset over a tropical archipelago!

5. Set the pot — start brewing the treasure broth!

Pour water into a pot and put it on the fire (an adult will do this!). When the water boils, add the carrots and garlic. Cook for a few minutes — until the carrots soften a bit. The smell is like an evening breeze by the shore!

6. Add the mussels — the treasure crew on board!

When the carrots are almost ready — add the mussels. If they are in shells, cook for 5–7 minutes until the shells open. If cleaned — 3–4 minutes is enough. All shells should open — discard those that remain closed. This is how pirates checked if the food was safe!

7. Add the nori — the secret ingredient from the ocean depths.

Tear the nori sheet into small pieces and throw it into the pot. They will slightly melt in the soup, adding a sea aroma. Nori is not just a seaweed, but a sea seasoning of pirate legends!

8. The final touches — sauce and aromatic oil.

Add soy sauce, a drop of sesame oil, salt, and pepper to taste. Mix everything — now the soup smells like a fresh wind over a sea of spices!

9. Serving — like a pirate elixir of strength!

Pour the soup into deep bowls. Sprinkle with greens on top. It can be served with boiled rice or a piece of bread. When you take a spoon — imagine you are in the pirate port of Haiphong or Macau, where sea brothers share dishes and stories!

10. Warning from Admiral Cambuzia:

— The steam is hot! Do not open the lid yourself — this is an adult's task.
— Do not eat the shells if they have not opened — this is the rule of all sea cooks.
— Work carefully with the knife and garlic and ask for help.
— Always wash your hands after preparing seafood.

Done! Mussel and nori soup — your magical broth for strength, wisdom, and new adventures!

This is not just a soup, but a piece of ancient coastal traditions: light, tasty, and full of the salty spirit of the sea. Pirates ate such a soup before a new raid because it gave strength, like a good sail — speed.

Bon appétit, young captain! Today your spoon is the helm!

Honey-Soy Tuna: The Golden Treasure from the Eastern Seas!

1. Ahoy, young culinary pirate! It's time to prepare a dish with the shine of gold!

Today, we are making honey-soy tuna — a dish considered elite even by the most discerning captains! It was prepared at festive parties in the bays of Siam and Hong Kong. Put on your apron, call your adult navigator — and let's fry the golden tuna to pirate songs!

2. Ingredients — the culinary map to golden taste:

Prepare:
— 2 pieces of tuna (100–150 g each, thick as a deck plank)
— 2 tablespoons of honey
— 2 tablespoons of soy sauce
— 1 teaspoon of lemon or lime juice
— ½ teaspoon of sesame oil (optional)
— a bit of black pepper
— oil for frying
— sesame seeds or green onions for garnish

3. **Preparing the marinade — like an elixir for sea treasures!**

In a bowl, mix honey, soy sauce, lemon or lime juice, a bit of pepper, and sesame oil. Stir with a spoon — the aroma will become sweet and salty, like adventures in the eastern spice market. This is the magic of taste that pirates of Singapore loved!

4. **Marinating the tuna — preparing the fish for a great journey!**

Place the tuna pieces in the marinade and leave for 15–20 minutes. Turn several times to ensure each side absorbs the flavors well. During this time, you can imagine yourself in the port of Macau, where chefs rubbed fish with spices before setting out to sea.

5. **The pan — our pirate stove!**

Ask an adult to heat a pan with a bit of oil. The heat should be medium. Place the tuna and fry for 2–3 minutes on each side. It should become golden on the outside but juicy inside, like the secret of a treasure chest. Don't overcook — tuna doesn't like long captivity!

6. **Thickening the marinade — a treasure sauce for the finish!**

Pour the remaining marinade into a small saucepan or pan. Boil over low heat for 2–3 minutes — it will thicken slightly. This will be our sauce — sweet, shiny, like the sun over the ocean.

7. **Serving — a pirate buffet in honor of a great victory!**

Place the tuna on a plate, drizzle with warm sauce. Sprinkle with sesame seeds or chopped green onions. It can be served with rice, vegetables, or even tropical fruits. Such a dish is like a sail on a festive ship!

8. **Secrets from the navigators of taste:**

— Want it more tender? Marinate the fish longer — up to 1 hour in the refrigerator.
— Honey can be replaced with syrup or cane sugar.
— A drop of garlic juice or grated ginger will add spiciness.
— The sauce can be used as a glaze on chicken, etc. — it's a universal treasure!

9. **Warnings from Captain Safe Galley:**

— The pan is hot — never touch it without adult help!
— Honey is sticky — wash your hands after working with it.
— Be careful with raw fish — do not taste before frying.
— Always keep track of time — do not leave the tuna on the fire unattended.

10. **The most important thing — a pirate's heart in every piece!**

While cooking, imagine yourself on a ship: the wind in the sails, seagulls crying, and the captain (you!) preparing their signature dish. This tuna is not just delicious — it's legendary!
And there you have it: honey-soy tuna — a treasure that melts in your mouth!

It was prepared in the East when spice ships anchored and pirates came ashore to celebrate. This taste is like a story of travels, spices, and genuine smiles.

Bon appétit, captain of adventures! Until the next culinary raids!

Rice Balls with Octopus: Sea Pearls for a Pirate Feast!

1. **Yo-ho-ho, little cook! Let's prepare to mold delicious sea pearls!**

Today in the galley — a special task: we will make rice balls with octopus! Pirates ate this dish on the Eastern islands when they wanted something tasty, fun, and convenient for a snack on the go. It's like culinary treasures hidden in rice. Ready? Then let's go, to magical molding and deliciousness!

2. **Ingredients — the map to the flavor chest:**

Prepare:
— 2 cups of cooked rice (preferably sticky or short-grain)
— 150 g of boiled octopus (can be frozen, pre-thawed)
— 1 tablespoon of soy sauce
— 1 teaspoon of sesame oil (or a bit of olive oil)
— 1 teaspoon of grated ginger (optional)
— a pinch of salt
— nori sheet or greens for decoration
— wet hands (yes, yes, it's important!)

3. **Preparing the octopus — the inhabitant of sea caves!**

If the octopus is raw — ask an adult to boil it for 30–40 minutes until it becomes soft. If already boiled — just cut it into small pieces. Its taste is delicate and marine, like the breath of wind over coral reefs!

4. **Mixing the filling — a secret blend from the ocean depths.**

Mix the octopus pieces with soy sauce, a drop of sesame oil, and ginger. This is an aromatic filling that will give the balls a magical spicy taste. The filling should be juicy but not liquid — otherwise, the balls will fall apart like shells in a storm!

5. **Rice is the base: like sails for our edible ships.**

The cooked rice should be slightly warm and sticky. If it's too dry — sprinkle with water. If too liquid — cool it down. With wet hands, take a handful of rice, flatten it in your palm, place a spoonful of filling inside, and roll it into a ball. Like a true kitchen pirate!

6. **Forming the balls — like real pearls from a pirate's chest!**

Carefully form a round ball the size of a tangerine. If you want — wrap part of the ball with a strip of nori, like a pirate's belt! Make as many balls as will fit in the treasure chest (or on the plate).

7. **You can fry a little — like gilding a pirate coin!**

Want a crispy crust? Ask an adult to quickly fry the balls in a pan with a drop of oil until lightly golden. But even without frying, they are tasty, tender, like sea mist over a lagoon.

8. **Serving — a pirate feast in the port!**

Place the balls on a lettuce leaf or in a basket, like real pearls. Put a dipping sauce nearby: soy, honey-mustard, or sweet and sour. You can sprinkle with sesame seeds or greens. Take with your hands and taste — that's how pirates ate, sitting on barrels of spices!

9. **Secrets from culinary seafarers:**

— You can add grated cheese to the rice — the balls will become stretchy.
— If there are no octopuses — shrimp or even tuna will do.
— For a fun look, you can make eyes from nori and turn the balls into "little octopuses."
— The balls can be frozen and then reheated — convenient for a sea journey!

10. **Warning from Admiral Cambuzia:**

— Never cut the octopus yourself — trust an adult with this.
— A hot pan is not for pirate fingers!
— Hands should be clean because we are working with rice that will stick to everything!
— If something falls — don't worry! In a pirate kitchen, even failure is an adventure!

Done! Rice balls with octopus — edible treasures that bring the joy and power of the sea!

This is not just food, but a fun, tasty way to feel the breath of the East and learn to cook something special with your own hands. Now your kitchen is a tropical island of adventure, and you are a captain with taste!

Bon appétit, brave pirate! To new gastro-raids!

Dessert with Tapioca and Lychee: A Sweet Treasure from the Tropical Chest!

1. Ahoy, young sweet-toothed pirate! Prepare for a taste boarding!

Today we will prepare a real tropical dessert that was loved by captains and young sailors in the ports of Vietnam, Thailand, and Malaysia — *dessert with tapioca and lychee*! It is cool, sweet, and mysteriously transparent, like pearls from pirate depths. Put on your apron, take a spoon instead of a saber — and fight for the delicacy!

2. Treasure chest of ingredients — let's find the exotic!

Here's what to find in the holds:
— ½ cup of small pearl tapioca
— 2 cups of water
— 1 cup of coconut milk
— 1-2 tablespoons of sugar (to taste)
— 1 can of lychee (or fresh, if you're lucky!)
— a pinch of vanilla or vanilla sugar
— a few ice cubes or mint (for beauty and freshness)

3. Cooking tapioca — pearls from the tropical lagoon!

Pour water into a pot and bring to a boil. Add tapioca (carefully!) and cook on low heat for 10–15 minutes until it becomes transparent with a small white dot inside. Stir with a spoon to prevent the pearls from sticking together like a mermaid's necklace!

4. Rinse — like treasures after sea foam!

When the tapioca is ready, strain it through a sieve and rinse with cold water. It will cool down and become shiny, like real pearls from the tropical bottom. Let it "rest" a bit — sea treasures don't like haste!

5. Coconut sauce — like a tropical wave of tenderness!

In a small pot, heat coconut milk with sugar and vanilla. Do not boil — just make it warm and aromatic. Stir everything with a spoon. The smell is like a sweet breeze on the island's shore, where palms and spices grow!

6. **Assembling the dessert — building an edible island map!**

In transparent glasses (it's prettier!), put a spoonful of tapioca, a few lychees on top, a bit more tapioca, and then pour warm coconut sauce. You can garnish with a mint leaf or a slice of lime. Want it cold? Add an ice cube!

7. **Cooling — like a sea pause before a sweet adventure!**

Place the dessert in the refrigerator for 20–30 minutes. It will become thicker, more tender, and refreshing — just what you need after a hot battle with lunch! But if you don't want to wait — enjoy it warm, like pirates did at night on the shore!

8. **Serve — like a festive dessert at a pirate carnival!**

Place the glasses on a tray, decorate with colorful spoons, umbrellas, or even shells (for decoration!). This dessert is perfect for a party or family dinner. Small pearls in sweet sauce — it's a taste magic!

9. **Secrets of the sweet galley:**

— Do not overcook the tapioca — it will become sticky.
— If the lychee is too sweet — you can add a few berries or a piece of banana.
— Instead of vanilla, you can add a pinch of cinnamon — for new adventures.
— Want color? Add pieces of mango or strawberries!

10. **Warning from the pirate confectioner:**

— Hot pot — only with the help of an adult!
— Do not boil coconut milk — it can escape like a cunning dolphin!
— Do not swallow hot tapioca — wait until it cools down!
— And don't forget: the tastiest is when you cook with a good mood and a bit of imagination!

Done! Dessert with tapioca and lychee — a sweet treasure at the bottom of the tropical heart!

This dessert is tender, like the song of waves, sweet, like adventures in the tropics, and light, like the breath of the sea. It was prepared at festive banquets when the ship returned from a successful raid. And now you have a real dessert with a pirate heart.

Bon appétit, captain! To new sweet discoveries!

English Privateers

1. **Breakfast on the Foggy Sea: Salty Cod Pie and Oats.**

English privateers — pirates with royal permission — started the day with a hearty meal to have enough strength for sea adventures. One of their favorite breakfasts was "fish pie" with salted cod, potatoes, and cream, if the ship had supplies. They often ate oatmeal (even with fish broth!) or "hardtack" — hard sea biscuit with a drop of lemon juice to prevent scurvy. The drink was strong tea or low-alcohol beer, safer than regular water on board.

2. **Soup from the Sea's Soul: Fish Stew "Sea Stew".**

For lunch, privateers prepared a simple but hearty fish stew. The pot included leftovers of sea fish — cod, haddock, hake, plus dried peas, potatoes, onions, sometimes carrots. This "sea stew" or "fish chowder" was cooked right on the deck in a large cauldron. The broth was thick, spicy, with pepper, bay leaf, and sometimes... an apple! Such a dish warmed on rainy days and lifted spirits before a raid.

3. **Main Course: Baked Fish with Flatbreads and Beans.**

For dinner, privateers could afford something special — baked cod or mackerel with dried herbs, if there was a catch or trophy. It was served with "pease pudding" — pea puree or stewed beans, as well as sea flatbreads — bread made from oat flour or dry barley cake. The food was often wrapped in linen napkins to keep it warm. The wind howls, the seagull cries — and in hand, a warm piece of fish!

4. **Side Dishes: Stewed Cabbage, Carrots, and Vegetable Stew.**

With the fish, they most often prepared stewed cabbage or carrots with herbs. If lucky, the ship had supplies of turnips, onions, or pumpkins. All this went into a simple vegetable stew or "bubble and squeak" — fried leftovers of vegetables from dinner. Privateers knew how to preserve food: they dried herbs, salted vegetables, and even fermented cabbage for long journeys.

5. **Sea Snack: Dried Fish and "Potted Shrimp".**

When they wanted a snack, privateers took out dried cod or herring. But in ports, a special snack was "potted shrimp" — small shrimps in spices and butter, stored in clay pots. They ate them with bread or just with a spoon, washed down with a warm drink. It was a true sea luxury, saved for a special evening.

6. **Drinks: Grog, Tea, and Lemon Water for Scurvy.**

To avoid scurvy, privateers drank water with lemon juice — this was called "lime ration". For adults, there was grog — diluted rum with water and lemon. But the favorite was hot tea with milk and cane sugar, when possible. It united the crew, warmed them, and inspired them to plan new sea maneuvers.

7. **Desserts for the Captain: Apple Pudding and Ginger Biscuits.**

Sweets were a rarity, but on special occasions, privateers made "duff" — boiled pudding with dried fruits, sometimes with apples or molasses. They also valued ginger cookies, which did not spoil for a long time and had a warming taste. Some ship bakers even baked small "ship's biscuits" with caraway and honey for the cabin boy — as a reward for good deck cleaning!

8. **Communal Dinner — A Ritual of Honor and Brotherhood.**

After each successful raid or storm, privateers held a communal dinner. Everyone sat on the deck, shared fish, bread, sometimes — grog. The captain shared plans or old tales, and someone tapped a spoon on a barrel instead of a drum. It was more than food — it was a moment of unity when everyone knew: we are a team, and every piece of fish here is honestly earned.

9. **Supplies for a Long Journey: Salted Fish and Bags of Biscuits.**

On board, there was always a supply: salted cod, barrels of herring, bags of "hardtack", dried apples or pears. Sometimes even dried peas in cloth bags. Privateers knew: supplies are not a luxury, but life. Food was stored in the holds, where it was cool, sometimes even hidden in special chests to avoid being found by rats or cabin boys with a healthy appetite.

10. **Privateers' Cuisine — Simple Dishes with a Taste of Adventure.**

The food of English privateers was simple, nutritious, and clever. They cooked with what they had, but did it with imagination: spices from India, fish from the English Channel, tea from Ceylon — all mixed in a pirate cauldron. These dishes are not just sustenance, but part of a great maritime history, where every spoonful of soup is like a piece of a map to the next treasure.

The cuisine of English privateers is a journey through time: between storms, teapots, salted fish, and sweet dreams. It teaches that even in the simplest biscuit, there can be a story, and together — even the humblest dinner becomes a true feast. Raise your spoons, privateers! The sea adventure continues!

Fish Soup "Sea Stew": A Cod Lunch for a True Privateer!

1. **Yo-ho-ho! Let's cook a real "Sea Stew" like the English privateers in the North Sea!**

Hello, young privateer! Ready to cook a magical sea soup that warmed captains and sailors during a storm? Fish soup "Sea Stew" is a warm, thick soup made from sea cod and vegetables, cooked in a cauldron or pot, just like on a pirate galley. Before you start, ensure safety — call an adult helper to assist with the knife and stove.

2. **Ingredient list — like a map to taste!**

You will need:
— 300 g of sea cod fillet (or other white fish)
— 1 potato
— 1 carrot
— 1 onion
— 1 celery stalk
— 1 clove of garlic
— 2 tablespoons of tomato paste
— 1 bay leaf
— 1 liter of water or fish broth
— a bit of olive oil
— salt, pepper, a pinch of dried thyme

3. **Preparing the vegetables is as important as preparing the ship for battle.**

Peel the potato, carrot, onion, and celery. Cut everything into cubes (the size of a doubloon — not too small). Remember: the more even the pieces, the tastier the soup will be! Simply crush the garlic with a knife — its aroma should be pirate-strong!

4. **Let's start cooking — pot on the stove!**

In a large pot, heat a bit of oil. Carefully add the onion, carrot, and celery. Sauté for 3-4 minutes, stirring with a wooden spoon. Then add the garlic and tomato paste — it gives the broth the color of the evening sea. Sauté for another minute.

5. **Time to add water and spices.**

Pour hot water or fish broth over the vegetables (you can use a cube, but true privateers cooked with heads and bones!). Add the bay leaf and a pinch of thyme. Salt and pepper. After boiling, reduce the heat and let it simmer for 15 minutes. This is the time when the vegetables "mature for the journey"!

6. **Fish on board!**

Now add the cod. Cut the fillet into large pieces (like sea rocks!) and gently place them in the soup. Cook for another 7–10 minutes. Do not stir too much — the fish is tender like sea foam and may fall apart. It should just gently simmer in the broth, absorbing the aroma of spices and vegetables.

7. **Thickness like the fog in the English Channel!**

To make the soup thicker, you can crush a few pieces of potato right in the pot — this is an old privateer trick. Some sailors also added breadcrumbs or baked bread — so the dish could be eaten with a spoon even during a storm!

8. **Final touch — taste like a captain.**

Remove the bay leaf (no one wants to chew leaves instead of fish!) and pour the soup into deep bowls. Sprinkle with herbs if you like. Bread or crackers go perfectly with the soup — pirates used them to scoop the thick broth straight from the pot!

9. **Tips from the chef-captain:**

— Do not over-fry the vegetables — then the soup will be sweet, not bitter.
— Use fresh fish — the broth will be more aromatic.
— If there is no cod, use hake or pangasius.
— For spiciness, you can add a pinch of paprika (but be careful — not all privateers liked it hot!).

10. **Warnings from the kitchen helmsman:**

Do not touch the hot pot without a potholder — it is as hot as a pirate's heart after a battle! And remember: only an adult helper works with knives! A true privateer is one who knows how to be brave *and* careful!

"Sea Stew" is not just a soup, but a real adventure in every spoonful!

As you savor it, imagine how English privateers hid from the storm somewhere in a bay, shared the last cod, warmed their hands over the pot... And with every sip, you become a little more of a cook, a little more of a sailor — and a true captain of your own culinary ship.

Salmon and Spinach Pie: A Meal for the Pirate Watch!

1. Hey-hey, young privateer! We're making a pie like on board the "Fearsome Seagull"!

English privateers knew: a delicious pie is the best weapon against fatigue and gloomy weather! Today we will learn how to make a salmon and spinach pie — hearty, fragrant, with a crispy crust, suitable for both celebrations and a picnic on the shore. Before you step onto the culinary deck, call your assistant sailor (that is, an adult), because we will be working with the oven!

2. Ingredients — like treasures from different ports!

You will need:
— 1 sheet of ready-made puff pastry (store-bought is fine)
— 150 g of salmon fillet (boiled or baked)
— 1 handful of fresh spinach (or frozen, thawed, and squeezed)
— 1 egg
— 2 tablespoons of cream cheese or sour cream
— a bit of cheese (hard or feta)
— salt, pepper, nutmeg (a pinch)
— a little flour for rolling out the dough
— oil or butter for frying the spinach

3. Thaw the dough — because it doesn't like to be rushed!

Take the puff pastry out of the fridge 20 minutes before cooking. Thawed dough is as elastic as a sail in a light breeze! Sprinkle the table with flour when rolling it out to prevent sticking — an old trick of ship bakers!

4. Prepare the filling — a real treasure inside!

Sauté the spinach in a drop of oil for 2-3 minutes until it reduces in volume. Ask an adult to help with the stove. Mix the salmon, spinach, cream cheese, grated cheese, a bit of salt, pepper, and a pinch of nutmeg in a bowl. Mash everything with a spoon. If the salmon is in large pieces, tear it with your hands, like a true captain dividing a treasure map!

5. Roll out the dough — like a map to the treasure island!

On a floured surface, roll out the dough to the thickness of a coin. You can make one large pie or several small ones, like portioned rations for pirates. Grease the form with butter or line it with parchment — so nothing sticks to the ship's bottom!

6. Fill the dough — like a cargo hold.

Place the filling in the center, leaving some space at the edges. If it's a large pie, cover with a second layer of dough and pinch the edges (you can use your fingers or a fork). If small, fold the dough like a letter and tightly seal the edges so the filling doesn't escape during the oven's sea battle!

7. Brush with the wind — glaze with egg for shine!

Beat the egg in a bowl and brush the top of the pie. This will make it golden, like a chest of doubloons. If desired, you can make small cuts on top — for beauty and to let steam out, like from a ship's smokestack.

8. Send to the oven — the pie sails on its voyage!

Place the pie in a preheated oven at 180°C. Bake for 20-25 minutes, or until the dough is golden. Ask an adult to monitor — the oven is as hot as a volcanic island!

9. Wait and cool — because you can't bite into a hot pie!

Take the pie out and let it cool a bit (10 minutes) — so you don't burn your tongue, like after a cannon battle! Then cut and serve on plates. Serve with a light salad or on its own — it's hearty and delicious, like a captain's dinner after a successful raid!

10. Tips from the ship's baker:

— If the dough tears, patch it with your hands, like a pirate mending sails.
— The filling shouldn't be too runny — otherwise, it will leak.
— You can experiment with the filling: add some corn, boiled egg, or green peas!
— Bake in the middle of the oven — and don't open the door too often!

Here is your Salmon and Spinach Pie — a royal meal for the captain!

It's hearty, aromatic, easy to make, and very tasty. Such a pie was enjoyed by English privateers on sea voyages — especially during calm evenings when the stars were visible in the sky, and the ship was rocked by the waves. Now you too are the master of the culinary rum!

Fried Cod in Batter: The Golden Fish of the Privateers!

1. Hey, young privateer! Today we're catching cod — and frying it in batter!

English privateers loved fried fish, especially cod! Crispy on the outside, soft and juicy on the inside — it became a favorite dish of many sailors. Today, we'll prepare it just like they did in the port taverns of Bristol or Liverpool. But first — safety! Ask an adult helper to be nearby, as we'll be frying in hot oil.

2. Gathering ingredients — the sea shopping list!

We need:
— 2 cod fillets (boneless)
— 5 tablespoons of flour (for the batter)
— 1 egg
— 100 ml of water or milk
— a pinch of salt
— a bit of lemon juice
— oil for frying (sunflower or canola)
— additional flour for coating the fish

3. **Prepare the fish — like a real ship for a voyage!**

Rinse the fish and pat it dry with a paper towel. If the fillet is large, cut it into smaller pieces suitable for frying. Add a little salt and sprinkle with lemon juice. Leave it for 10 minutes to marinate a bit. By the way, lemon is not only tasty but also helps combat the smell of the sea!

4. **Prepare the batter — a foamy shirt for the fish!**

In a bowl, mix the flour with a pinch of salt. Add the egg, then water or milk, and mix well with a whisk or fork until there are no lumps. The batter should be like liquid sour cream — not too thick, but not like water either. This is the armor for the fish to make it crispy and golden.

5. **Coat and dip — the secret to a golden coating!**

First, coat each piece of fish in flour — this will help the batter stick better. Then carefully dip it into the bowl with the batter. Let it drip a bit — the batter shouldn't flow like a river, or it will be too thick.

6. **The pan — like a hot deck, be careful!**

Heat a pan with plenty of oil on the stove — so the fish swims like in the sea. Check the temperature by dropping a bit of batter: if it sizzles immediately, it's time to fry! Ask an adult to place the fish in the pan to avoid burns.

7. **Fry to golden victory!**

Each piece is fried for 3–4 minutes on each side. Don't flip too often — it's better to wait until the bottom becomes crispy. When the fish is ready, place it on a paper towel to drain excess oil. This is an old trick from the port kitchen!

8. **Secrets of true privateers:**

— Want a fluffier batter? Add a pinch of baking powder.
— For an interesting taste, add a bit of ground garlic or herbs.
— Don't put all the fish in at once — the oil will cool down, and the batter won't be crispy.
— If there's no cod, substitute with hake or pangasius.

9. **Serve like in a tavern!**

Serve the fried cod with mashed potatoes or baked potatoes, or even better — with sweet and sour sauce, pea puree, or just with lemon. You can add some greens on top for beauty and freshness.

10. **Remember the rules of sea safety!**

The oil is very hot — don't touch it with your hands, even if it seems to have cooled down. Don't approach the stove alone, and don't leave it unattended. The pan is like a pirate cannon: strong, hot, and requires experience!

Here is your fried cod in batter — the golden fish of the captain's menu!

When the crispy batter crunches in your mouth, and the tender fish melts — you're definitely on board a real English privateer ship, somewhere off the coast of Cornwall. The dish is simple but delicious — just like pirates loved after a long voyage. Enjoy, young culinary captain!

Sea Shepherd's Pie: A Privateer's Tale in a Pot!

1. **Welcome, young privateer! Today we're making Sea Shepherd's Pie!**

In the distant turbulent times, English privateers invented a special dish — *shepherd's pie*, but with a maritime character. Instead of meat — fish, instead of a shepherd — a sailor! This pie is a tender fish stew under a fluffy blanket of mashed potatoes. Aromatic, hearty, and warming — perfect for a cold evening on a ship or at home. Ready? Hoist the sails — we're going on a culinary boarding!

2. **Provisions from the galley — here's what you need:**

— 300 g of white fish fillet (cod, hake, or pangasius)
— 2 potatoes
— 1 carrot
— 1 small onion
— 1/2 cup of milk
— 1 tablespoon of butter
— 1 tablespoon of flour
— 1/2 cup of grated cheese (optional)
— salt, pepper
— herbs for garnish (optional)

3. **Preparing the fish — how to get cod ready for a sea voyage.**

You can first slightly boil the fish in salted water or steam for 5–7 minutes. Then cool and divide into pieces — not too small, so the fish feels like a real sea treasure in the pie. If there are bones — ask an adult to remove them!

4. **Making the "waves" — fluffy mashed potatoes!**

Peel the potatoes, cut into pieces, and boil until soft (20 minutes). Drain the water, add a bit of butter, milk, salt — and mash to a soft puree. You can use a fork or a special masher. The puree should be airy, like clouds over the ocean.

5. **Vegetable outpost — carrot and onion on guard of flavor.**

Finely chop the onion, grate the carrot. Ask an adult to fry everything in a spoonful of oil for 3–5 minutes, until soft. Add flour to them, mix, and gradually pour in some milk — a gentle sauce will form. It will bind the fish with the vegetables into a single pirate story!

6. **All together — assembling the pie in a port pot.**

In a mold (or a deep bowl that can withstand the oven), first lay out the vegetable sauce with fish. Carefully smooth it out. On top, lay the mashed potatoes — with a spoon or spatula, as if spreading clouds on a sea map. If you want — sprinkle grated cheese on top for a crispy crust.

7. Into the oven — let it bake like under the sun in the tropics!

Place the form in the oven, preheated to 180°C. Bake for 20 minutes, or until the top becomes slightly golden. If adding cheese — you can bake a little longer to form an aromatic pirate "crust"!

8. While the pie is baking — pirate tips from the galley:

— If there's no fish, you can mix with canned tuna.
— Add a bit of green peas or corn — it will be brighter!
— Cheese is not mandatory, but with it, the pie tastes royal.
— It's better to grease the form with butter so nothing sticks.

9. Be careful with the hot, because even the sea sometimes burns!

Ask an adult to take the form out of the oven. It's very hot — don't touch without gloves! Let the pie cool for 5–10 minutes — it will firm up a bit, and the taste will be even better.

10. Serve — and present as on a captain's table!

Serve the pie with a spoon directly from the form, garnished with a sprig of greenery. Eat with a spoon, sipping milk or tea, and imagine how English privateers feasted on such a dish after capturing an enemy frigate!

Sea Shepherd's Pie — a dish of heart, strength, and salty legends!

You have just prepared something special — a dish where the warmth of potatoes, the tenderness of fish, and the spirit of English ports come together! Its taste is like a good sea story: warming, inspiring, and you want more. Bravo, captain — you have a true culinary compass!

Herring with Onions: A Pirate Delicacy in a Barrel!

1. Hello, young privateer! Today we are not frying, but marinating!

In distant sea voyages, it was difficult to preserve fresh fish. That's why pirates and privateers marinated it — especially herring! This fish, marinated with onions, was a favorite treat in port taverns. Its taste is salty, spicy, and a bit tangy, like a wave during a storm. And although it's a dish that isn't eaten immediately, its preparation is a true culinary adventure!

2. **Marinating treasures — what we need:**

— 2 herring fillets
— 1 large onion
— 150 ml of water
— 2 tablespoons of vinegar (preferably apple or wine)
— 1 teaspoon of sugar
— 3–4 black peppercorns
— 1 bay leaf
— a few allspice berries
— a jar with a tight lid (no barrels — a glass fleet will do!)

3. **Herring — the main fish on board!**

If your herring is very salty, it should first be soaked in water for 1–2 hours (ask an adult to help with this). Then rinse, pat dry with a napkin, and cut into pieces — the size of a privateer's coin. This will be our main hero in the jar.

4. **Onion — a sea decoration and aromatic friend of herring.**

Peel the onion (don't cry, privateer!) and cut into thin rings. If it's very sharp — scald it with boiling water to make it softer. This is an old pirate trick to avoid an "onion storm" in your mouth!

5. **Preparing the marinade — pirate brine.**

In a saucepan, mix water, vinegar, sugar, bay leaf, pepper, and allspice. Put on the heat and bring to a boil. Then remove from heat and cool — it's important not to pour hot marinade over the fish, as it will become boiled, not marinated!

6. **Layering everything in the jar — like treasures in a chest.**

In a clean jar, layer: a little onion, pieces of herring, onion again. Repeat until all ingredients are used up. Then pour the cooled marinade — to cover everything inside! Close with a lid, but not too tightly, let it "breathe" a little on the first day.

7. Time — the main spice of the pirate recipe!

Place the jar in the refrigerator for 24 hours. During this time, the herring will absorb the spicy aroma, the onion will soften, and the marinade will work its magic. The next day — open and serve!

8. Marinating secrets from the ship's boatswain:

— If you want a slightly sweeter marinade — add another half teaspoon of sugar.
— You can add a little mustard or mustard seeds — for more piquancy.
— For color — a ring of carrot or beet (but then the marinade will turn pink!).
— Herring tastes better on the second and third day — don't rush!

9. Safety first in the galley!

Only an adult works with a knife. Hot marinade — don't touch! And it's also important: the jar must be well washed before use, otherwise pirate bacteria will invade the sea of taste!

10. Tasting — like a real sailor in port!

Serve herring with black bread, boiled potatoes, or egg. You can also garnish with greens — and it will be a real captain's treat. Eat with a fork, slowly, as if deciphering a treasure map on the Island of Taste!

Herring with onions — a dish with character, like a true pirate!

Marinated, tangy, aromatic — it tastes especially good after waiting. Just like adventures at sea: the best ones are worth waiting for. Now your culinary diary has another delicious story. Bravo, privateer!

Crab Salad with Apple: A Fresh Treasure on the Privateer's Table!

1. Hello, young privateer! Today we are making a salad that even a sea crab wouldn't be afraid of!

English privateers, although known for their love of hearty food, occasionally indulged in fresh dishes with a light sea flavor. Crab salad with apple is a true pirate's balance: tender, slightly sweet, and a bit crunchy! It's easy to prepare, but there are some culinary tricks. And remember: a privateer always works with neatness and caution, as with real treasures!

2. What you need for the salad — like a map with ingredients:

— 100–150 g of crab sticks (or crab meat, if you're lucky!)
— 1 green apple (Granny Smith type)
— 1 boiled egg
— 1 tablespoon of mayonnaise or yogurt
— a bit of lemon juice
— salt to taste
— greens (parsley or dill)
— a bowl — your navigator's vessel!

3. Crab sticks — not real claws, but tasty!

Ask an adult to help you cut the crab sticks into small cubes or strips. If you're using real crab meat, shred it with your fingers or a fork. Pirates valued seafood, even if it had to be caught... in a supermarket!

4. Apple — a fresh friend on a sea journey!

Peel the apple (or leave it if it's tender) and grate it on a large grater or cut into thin strips. Sprinkle the apple with a few drops of lemon juice — this will keep it fresh and white. Lemon is a pirate's preservative, tested in long voyages!

5. Egg — the golden trophy of the sailor's chicken!

Peel the boiled egg and cut it into cubes or grate it. This will make the salad more tender and the taste richer. By the way, eggs on ships were kept like pearls — because they were not often found in the open sea!

6. **Mix all the ingredients in one bowl — the schooner of taste!**

Put the crab sticks, apple, and egg in the bowl. Add a little mayonnaise or yogurt — not too much, the salad shouldn't float like a boat in a storm! A bit of salt, a spoon of green magic (parsley or dill) — and it's ready!

7. **Ship presentation — the captain eats with his eyes!**

Serve the salad in small portioned plates or shells (if you find decorative ones!). You can serve it on a lettuce leaf or in half an apple with the core removed. Even pirates liked to eat beautifully when there was no storm.

8. **Tips from the galley master:**

— Don't add too much sauce — the salad will lose its lightness.
— You can add a little corn for a sweet accent.
— Try it without salt — sometimes crab sticks are salty enough.
— Want to make it more interesting? Use orange slices instead of apple!

9. **Warning for the young pirate:**

Work with a knife and grater only with an adult — the crab doesn't bite, but you can easily nick a finger! Don't drip lemon juice in your eyes — a pirate must be careful even with citrus storms!

10. **Tasting — like a picnic on a deserted island!**

Crab salad with apple is best when it has rested a bit in the cold. Put it in the fridge for 10–15 minutes — and then serve. It's a refreshing dish for a light pirate lunch or a snack between boardings!

Crab salad with apple — light as a sail and fresh as a northern breeze!

This is not just a salad, but a real sea surprise in every spoon! It proves that pirate food is not only fatty and hot but also light, healthy, and interesting. Now there's another treasure in your culinary chest. Bon appétit, captain!

Mussel Soup with Cream and Thyme: Pirate Tenderness in Every Spoon!

1. Hello, young privateer! We are preparing for soup navigation!

Mussels are a true treasure from the ocean floor. English privateers loved adding them to soups, especially during stops near rocky shores. This creamy soup with thyme is tender, aromatic, and very maritime. It's easy to prepare if you have an experienced elder nearby — because mussels, though delicious, require attention. Let's start our culinary voyage!

2. Provisions from the hold — here's what you need:

— 500 g of fresh mussels in shells (or 200 g of cleaned frozen ones)
— 1 tablespoon of butter
— 1 small onion
— 1 clove of garlic
— 200 ml of cream (10–20%)
— 300 ml of water or fish broth
— 1 sprig of fresh or ½ tsp of dried thyme
— salt, pepper
— bread or croutons for serving
— and of course — a helper sailor, that is, an adult!

3. Preparing the mussels — like cleaning the deck!

If the mussels are in shells, rinse them well under cold water. If you notice an open shell that doesn't close when touched, discard it (it's spoiled). It's best to clean the shells with a brush or a blunt knife — just like real pirates cleaned the deck of shells after fishing!

4. We start with sautéing — like heating the galley in calm weather.

Melt the butter in a pot. Add finely chopped onion and garlic, sauté a bit until they become translucent. This is the first aroma of the soup — and it should be gentle, like a breeze from the bay.

5. **Time to launch the mussels — like dropping anchor in a delicious bay!**

Add the mussels to the pot and cover with a lid. Simmer for 3–5 minutes until the shells open. Didn't open? Discard them. They are like closed chests — if they didn't open in battle, they are not worth tasting.

6. **We drain the treasure — making the broth.**

Carefully remove the mussels (an adult can help), and leave the juice they released in the pot — this will be the base of the soup. Add water or fish broth, thyme, and bring to a gentle boil. The aroma will be such as if you are standing on the edge of a cliff above the ocean!

7. **We add cream — the pirate elixir of tenderness!**

When the soup boils, pour in the cream, stir, and reduce the heat. Cook for 5 minutes on low heat to let everything combine. Don't let the cream boil too much — because the sea should be calm, not turbulent!

8. **We return the mussels home — to the soup harbor.**

You can leave the shells whole (they are beautiful!) or remove the meat and return only it — it will be easier to eat. This depends on you and your helper! Salt and pepper the soup to taste. Try a spoonful — if you want more aroma, add a little more thyme.

9. **Serving on the captain's table!**

Pour the soup into deep bowls, garnish with a sprig of greens or a slice of lemon. Serve with crispy bread or croutons — privateers used them to soak up the creamy broth to the last drop. Eat carefully — and enjoy every sip, like the starry sky above the ship.

10. **Tips and warnings from the boatswain:**

— Keep only those mussels that opened after cooking.
— Always wash your hands after working with seafood.
— Don't leave the soup on the heat for too long — the cream might escape.
— Mussels spoil quickly — always check them before cooking!

Mussel soup with cream — a tender journey in every spoon!

This is not just a dish, but a true sea adventure. It's light, healthy, and warms the soul. English privateers might have eaten such a soup before setting sail into the fog or after a long watch. And now you too — a young sailor with taste! Bon voyage and full spoons!

Barley Porridge with Shrimp: A Pirate's Lunch Between Storm and Calm!

1. **Hello, young privateer! It's time to cook porridge that even the captain would be proud to serve!**

On long voyages, English privateers often took barley with them because it stored well, wasn't afraid of salty air, and was quite filling. And when you add shrimp to barley, you get a pirate dish, somewhere between a soup and a porridge: soft, fragrant, and a bit sea-like. Perfect for warming up after a watch or during a rain on the deck!

2. **Ingredients — the ship's cargo:**

— ½ cup of pearl barley
— 1 carrot
— 1 small onion
— 1 tablespoon of oil or butter
— 100–150 g of cooked or frozen shrimp
— 3 cups of water or vegetable broth
— a pinch of salt, pepper
— herbs for garnish (dill, parsley)
— a slice of lemon (optional)

3. **The main character — barley! Let's prepare it properly.**

Barley or pearl barley should first be rinsed well and then soaked in water for at least 2 hours (or overnight). This will make the grains soft, and the dish will cook faster. Soaked barley is like a well-weathered sail: it listens to the fire!

4. **The vegetable crew — carrot and onion to the rescue!**

Cut the carrot into small cubes and the onion even smaller. Ask an adult to help with the knife. Then sauté everything in oil or butter in a pot for 5–6 minutes until golden and aromatic. This will be a tasty "wake" for the porridge!

5. **Add the barley and pour in — the boiling adventure begins!**

Drain the water in which the barley was soaked and add it to the sautéed vegetables. Pour in 3 cups of water or broth. Bring to a boil, reduce the heat, and simmer on low heat under a lid for 30–40 minutes, stirring occasionally. If the liquid evaporates, add more. The mixture should resemble a runny porridge or thick soup — just like a pirate's!

6. **Shrimp on deck!**

When the barley is almost ready (soft but holding its shape), add the peeled shrimp. If they are raw, boil for 5–7 minutes. If already cooked, 2–3 minutes will suffice. Don't overcook! Shrimp are as tender as pirate songs at sunset.

7. **The final touches — spices and love!**

Salt, pepper, and taste. If you wish, add a drop of lemon juice for a sea freshness. You can also add a pinch of dried thyme or dill. This will deepen the flavor, like the sea at full speed.

8. **Serving — like at a captain's feast!**

Pour the porridge into deep plates. Garnish with herbs or a slice of lemon on the side. Serve with croutons or a piece of black bread. The porridge is thick, aromatic, but moderately runny — to be eaten with a spoon, like a true sailor in the cold wind!

9. **Tips from the galley master:**

— To make the barley soft and cook quickly, always soak it in advance.
— Don't be afraid to add more water — the dish should be tender.
— If there are no shrimp, you can substitute with pieces of cooked fish or even canned tuna.

10. **Warnings for the young sailor:**

Always cook near an adult, especially when working with a knife or stove. Hot porridge and steam can burn! Don't taste raw shrimp — they should be well-cooked, as pirates respect not only taste but also safety!

Barley porridge with shrimp — a warm harbor on a cold day!

This dish is like a sea adventure that starts with a vegetable breeze, sails on barley waves, and ends with tender shrimp in a port of creamy flavor. Bravo, privateer! Your dish is a true pirate's pride!

Tuna Paste Sandwiches: A Snack for a True Sea Scout!

1. **Hello, young privateer! We're making sandwiches — small portions of big flavor!**

In the adventurous life of privateers, there wasn't always time for a hot meal. But even in a short break between boardings, you could have a tasty snack! Tuna paste sandwiches are nutritious, quick, and very pirate-like! And most importantly, easy to make with your own hands. Let's go, put on a kitchen apron instead of a coat and get to work!

2. **Ingredients — treasures in the pantry:**

— 1 can of canned tuna (in its own juice or in oil)
— 1–2 tablespoons of mayonnaise or unsweetened yogurt
— ½ teaspoon of lemon juice
— a pinch of salt, pepper
— 1 teaspoon of mustard (optional)
— 1 boiled egg (optional)
— a few slices of bread (white, toast, rye — your choice)
— lettuce leaves, cucumber or tomato slices — for decoration

3. **Preparing the paste — the lubricant for the bread ship!**

Open the can of tuna (ask an adult for help if you need a knife or can opener). Drain the excess liquid. Place the tuna in a bowl and mash it with a fork until it resembles a paste. Add mayonnaise or yogurt, lemon juice, a pinch of salt, and pepper. Mix well. Want to add mustard or finely chopped boiled egg? Go ahead! It will make the taste deeper, like an underwater cave.

4. **Secret spice — lemon and privateer courage!**

Lemon juice adds freshness and a bit of acidity, which suits the tuna. But don't overdo it — otherwise, instead of paste, you'll have a sour wind from the north! It's better to add a few drops first and taste.

5. **Preparing the bread — the foundation of a pirate sandwich.**

You can use the bread as it is, or you can toast it in a toaster or on a dry pan — then it will be crispy, like an old map. Toasted bread holds the paste better and looks very "privateer-like".

6. **Spreading the paste — measured, like cargo in the hold!**

Spread the paste carefully with a spoon or knife (plastic — for safety). Not too thin — but not like a mountain of treasures either. Remember: nothing should fall overboard for pirates!

7. **Decorating — as if preparing for a banquet in the royal harbor!**

Place a lettuce leaf, a slice of cucumber, or tomato on top. You can sprinkle with chopped greens. The sandwiches look beautiful — like a frigate with flags before a parade!

8. Serve with mood — a pirate eats not only with the mouth but also with the eyes!

Arrange the sandwiches on a plate or board. You can cut them in half or diagonally — it will be more convenient to hold. If you have pirate toothpicks (or regular ones) — decorate them like pirate flags!

9. Privateer chef's tips:

— If the paste is too runny — add more tuna or a bit of chopped boiled egg.
— For aroma, you can add a pinch of paprika or green onion.
— Tuna in its own juice is lighter, while in oil — more intense. Choose like a pirate chooses a route — depending on the weather and mood!

10. Attention on board: warnings!

Don't touch metal openers yourself — call an adult. If working with a knife — only with a safe one! And always wash your hands before and after cooking — pirates also maintained hygiene (especially those who lived long)!

Tuna paste sandwiches — a dish for exploration, boarding, and a good mood!

They are prepared quickly, disappear even faster, and taste great at any time — even under the starry sky on the deck. Now your culinary diary has another recipe for true captains of taste. Enjoy, pirate!

Mackerel on the Grill with an Apple Note: A Smoky Masterpiece for the Gourmet Pirate!

1. Ahoy, young privateer! It's time to grill fish — just like they did in the smoky coves of the English Channel!

Mackerel is one of the favorite fish of English sailors: fatty, nutritious, and easy to catch near the coast. We'll add a spicy apple note to it — and it will become not just dinner, but a true maritime masterpiece. The grill replaces the campfire on the shore, and the recipe is a map to flavor. But don't forget: only an adult captain can work with fire!

2. **Sea Cargo — What We Need:**

— 1 mackerel (already cleaned or with the help of an adult)
— ½ apple (preferably tart-sweet, like a green one)
— 1 teaspoon of olive oil
— salt, pepper
— ½ teaspoon of lemon juice
— a few sprigs of thyme or rosemary (optional)
— foil or grill rack

3. **Preparing the Mackerel — Like Cleaning the Deck Before Battle!**

If the mackerel is whole, ask an adult to clean it of scales, remove the guts and gills. Rinse the fish under water and pat dry with a paper towel. Now it's ready for marinating — like a ship before sailing!

4. **Apple Stuffing — An Unexpected Treasure in the Fish!**

Slice the half apple into thin slices. Drizzle them with lemon juice to prevent browning. You can add a bit of chopped greens or a sprig of thyme. This will be the "stuffing" that gives the mackerel aroma and a light tartness — like apples from the coastal orchards of Cornwall!

5. **Salting, Peppering, and Oiling — Preparing for the Grill Boarding!**

Salt and pepper the fish on the outside and inside. Then brush it with oil so the skin is crispy and doesn't stick to the rack. Place the apple slices inside the belly — they will steam with the fish juice, adding a magical aroma.

6. **Wrapping in Foil or Placing on the Rack — Choose Your Route!**

There are two ways to grill mackerel:
— *In foil* — juicy, tender, and without the risk of burning.
— *On the rack* — a smokier taste and crispy skin (but requires an experienced adult captain). Choose the option with an adult and get ready for a delicious hunt!

7. **The Grill — It's Like the Kitchen's Cannon!**

An adult will help heat the grill to medium temperature. If you're cooking on a grill pan, heat it well. Mackerel cooks for 5–6 minutes on each side (or 10–12 minutes in foil). When the meat turns white and flakes easily, it's ready!

8. **Serving — Like a Feast at the Governor's!**

Carefully remove the fish from the grill. Place it on a plate, garnish with lemon slices, greens, or leave a few apple slices. Serve with baked potatoes, salad, or a piece of bread. And don't forget to serve it nicely — even pirates eat beautifully!

9. **Tips from Experienced Privateers:**

— The apple gives the fish a fruity note but won't make it sweet — don't worry!
— If you want more smoky aroma, add a wood chip or a sprig of rosemary to the grill.
— Don't flip the fish often — mackerel is as delicate as an old compass.
— If the mackerel is boneless (fillet), cook it faster because it's thinner!

10. **Warning for the Young Sailor!**

The grill is as hot as a cannonball — touching it alone is forbidden! All operations with fire, knives, and hot foil are only under the control of an adult captain. Also, don't put the fish straight from the fridge onto the fire, or it will jump like a dolphin!

Mackerel on the grill with an apple note is a dish for those who aren't afraid of adventures in taste!

This is a hot, aromatic dish with character: juicy fish, crispy skin, and a mysterious sweet and sour note inside. You've just prepared something that could be served in a tavern or at a captain's picnic! Bravo, young pirate — now you're not just a treasure hunter, but also a master of the fire of taste!

Fermented Cabbage Pirate-Style: A Vitamin Chest for Sea Voyages!

1. **Ahoy, young captain! Today we are not frying, not steaming, but magically fermenting!**

Pirates knew: long voyages are not just adventures, but challenges. To stay healthy at sea, you need vitamin reserves. The best dish for this is fermented cabbage! It's crunchy, healthy, and can last in a barrel even longer than a ship in port.

2. **Ingredient treasure chest — as simple as on an old frigate:**

Prepare:
— 1 medium head of cabbage (white)
— 1 carrot
— 1 tablespoon of non-iodized salt (regular rock or sea salt)
— a large bowl
— a clean glass jar or plastic container
— a wooden spoon (no sabers this time)

3. **Chop the cabbage — like shredding a treasure map!**

Cut the cabbage head in half (an adult should do this), then slice it into thin strips — as if preparing ribbons for pirate flags. The thinner, the better — the cabbage will start to "bubble" faster, like a storm in a bottle!

4. **Add the carrot — the color of the sun in a tropical storm!**

Grate the carrot on a large grater and add it to the cabbage. Mix everything — you're already creating a tasty supply that could be stored even in a ship's hold!

5. **Add salt — the magical key to fermentation!**

Add salt to the mixture. Now the magic begins: with your hands (clean!), start kneading the cabbage as if squeezing out sea waves

It should become softer and release juice — this is a sign that everything is going right. Do this for 5–10 minutes, with a pirate's smile and patience!

6. Pack it in a jar — like treasure in a bottle!

Place the cabbage in the jar, packing it tightly with a spoon or fist (carefully!). The juice should cover the cabbage on top — otherwise, it will get upset and spoil. If there's not enough juice, add a little boiled water with a pinch of salt.

7. Cover, cover — and leave in the bay of fermentation!

Do not close the jar tightly — just cover it with gauze or a lid without sealing. Place it in a warm place (but not in direct sunlight). The cabbage will start to "bubble" on the 2nd or 3rd day — it's having fun, like sailors after shore leave!

8. Take care of it like a ship at sea!

Every day, remove the foam with a spoon (it will appear — this is normal) and press the cabbage down a bit so it doesn't float. After 5–7 days, taste it — if it's crunchy, tangy, and delicious — it's ready! If you want a stronger flavor, leave it for a couple more days.

9. Transfer to the treasure chest — store in the refrigerator!

The ready cabbage can be sealed with a tight lid and stored in the refrigerator. It tastes great with sandwiches, porridge, or just with a spoon — pirates ate it even on night watches to be as strong as an anchor!

10. Warning from Captain Preservant:

— Never use metal objects that can oxidize.
— Make sure your hands and jars are clean — cabbage doesn't like dirt!
— Do not eat cabbage that has a strange smell or slime — it's no longer a treasure.
— And most importantly — don't rush. Flavor comes with time, like true adventures!

That's it, captain! Now you have your own fermented cabbage — a pirate vitamin preserve that saves from illness and adds strength for all culinary raids!

It was prepared even in storms, even without a refrigerator, and every bite was a bite of health and adventure. Now this tradition is in your hands!

Bon appétit, little sailor! Many delicious raids await ahead!

Bouillabaisse: The Pirate Fish Treasure from France!

1. Ahoy, young privateer! Today — not just a dish, but a *legend of the sea*!

Bouillabaisse is a French fish soup from Marseille, which privateers learned from local fishermen during their stops in the Mediterranean. It is made from pieces of various fish, vegetables, herbs, and spices. And although it sounds complicated — we will cook it together, step by step, so you become a true pirate chef. The main thing is to have patience, clean hands, and... one good adult helper!

2. Ingredients — the sea catch and gifts of the land:

— 300 g of fish (preferably several types: cod, hake, mackerel, or even pieces of red fish)
— 1 carrot
— 1 tomato or a spoonful of tomato paste
— 1 onion
— 1 clove of garlic
— 1 bay leaf
— ½ tsp of thyme (or Provençal herbs)
— 2 tablespoons of oil
— ½ liter of water or fish broth
— salt, pepper
— lemon zest (just a little, not sour!)
— bread or croutons for serving

3. Preparing the vegetables — reconnaissance before boarding!

Start with chopping: dice the onion, slice the carrot into rounds, mince the garlic. You can grate the tomato or use a bit of tomato paste. This will be the base of the soup — like a map before a journey, setting the direction.

4. We start with frying — on the galley fire!

Heat the oil in a pot. Add the onion, carrot, and garlic, and fry for a few minutes. Then add the tomato or paste. Everything should become soft and fragrant — like on a coastal kitchen somewhere in the port of Marseille.

5. Pouring in the water — the waves are coming!

Add water or broth, bay leaf, thyme, a bit of salt, and pepper. Bring to a boil, reduce the heat, and simmer for 10–15 minutes. This is the time when the aroma will start spreading, like sails in the sea!

6. Fish in the soup — the main character enters the stage!

Cut the fish into large cubes, carefully place it in the soup. If there are pieces of different fish — even better! Simmer on low heat for 10 minutes. Do not stir too much — the fish is delicate, like friendship with a French fisherman!

7. A little secret — lemon zest and love!

Add a bit of lemon zest (thinly peeled skin) — just a pinch! This will add freshness. In France, it was believed: if bouillabaisse is without zest — then it's not bouillabaisse, just a fish soup!

8. Serving — on a pirate table with French charm!

Pour the bouillabaisse into deep bowls. Serve with crispy bread or croutons, or better yet — rub a toast with garlic and serve it alongside (this is called "rouille" — an old Provençal serving). Carefully lay out the pieces of fish — and don't forget the greens on top!

9. **Captain's tips from Marseille:**

— Do not overcook the fish — it should remain tender.
— Thyme or "Provençal herbs" — an essential privateer touch.
— You can add some seafood (shrimp or mussels) if you want a sea flavor explosion!
— If you want a thicker soup — mash a few vegetables in the broth before adding the fish.

10. **Safety — above all, even in soup!**

Always cook with an adult nearby, especially when working with a knife or a hot pot. Do not taste raw fish. Remember: even the best privateers stayed away from the fire without the helmsman's permission!

Bouillabaisse — pirate warmth with a French character!

You have just prepared a dish that warmed sailors in any weather. Light, aromatic, with a deep sea flavor — this soup is not just food, but a part of history. Now you have the *secret of a Marseille friend* — keep it, privateer, and pass it on when it's your turn to be the chef on the galley!

Oatmeal on Fish Broth: Energy for a Privateer's Raid!

1. **Ahoy, young privateer! Today you will prepare a porridge that was eaten in the strongest storms!**

In distant voyages, privateers had few supplies but plenty of ingenuity. And so a special dish appeared — *oatmeal on fish broth*. Sounds strange? Not at all! It's a nutritious, slightly salty, surprisingly tasty dish that fills you up quickly and is perfect for breakfast or lunch on board. Prepare it — and you'll surprise even the ship's captain!

2. **What you need — supplies from the privateer's ship hold:**

— 1 cup of fish broth (can be from a cube, but better — real from fish bones)
— ½ cup of oatmeal (not instant!)
— 1 teaspoon of butter (or oil)
— a pinch of salt
— dill or green onion — for garnish (optional)
— a few pieces of boiled fish — if available (this is the privateer's luxury!)

3. Fish broth — like a clear sea in a bowl.

If you have real fish broth — great! If not, you can ask an adult to make it from fish bones or use half a cube. It's important that the broth is *clear*, without a lot of spices — as it's the base of the porridge, not a soup.

4. Porridge — it's simple if you focus like during a boarding!

Pour the broth into a saucepan and bring to a boil (together with an adult!). Add a pinch of salt. Then slowly pour in the oatmeal, stirring constantly to prevent clumping.

5. Simmer, don't rush — like during a calm sea.

Reduce the heat and cook for 5–7 minutes, stirring with a wooden spoon. The oatmeal will start to thicken, absorbing the flavor of the broth. If it seems too thick — add a little more broth or boiled water.

6. Butter — the final touch on the pirate's canvas!

When the porridge is ready, add a spoonful of butter. Stir — and it will melt like the sun over the sea. If you want, you can add a bit of boiled fish or even a piece of herring if you're as brave as a true captain!

7. Serving — simple but beautiful!

Spoon the porridge into a bowl. On top — green onion or dill, a bit of pepper, a piece of fish for decoration. It looks like a dish from a fisherman's tavern on the Scottish coast!

8. Galley tips:

— Oatmeal tastes better warm, but not hot.
— If the broth is very salty — don't add extra salt.
— For a more interesting flavor, you can add a drop of lemon juice or mustard seeds.
— You can try this porridge with buckwheat too — it will be a privateer's experiment!

9. **Warnings for the pirate cook:**

Work with the broth and hot saucepan only *together with an adult!* Never leave boiling porridge unattended — it escapes faster than a boat in a storm!

10. **Privateer's breakfast — simple, hearty, and with character!**

This porridge is for true pirates who aren't afraid of new flavors. It gives strength, warmth, and a bit of the sea in every spoonful. Savor it slowly — and imagine yourself in a port where seagulls cry and fishermen greet you, knowing: *this is the young privateer who cooks like a true sea wolf!*

Oatmeal on fish broth — unexpectedly delicious, nutritious, and boldly privateer-like!

Now your culinary diary has another special recipe — one that will surprise friends and strengthen the spirit. Bon appétit, captain, and remember: even the simplest dishes can become a legend if you add a bit of imagination and the sea in your heart!

Baked Cod or Mackerel with Dried Herbs: A Dish for the Captain at Anchor!

1. **Hello, young privateer! We are preparing for baking — like a sea stopover!**

After stormy days at sea, English privateers loved a calm dinner. And nothing was tastier than *baked cod or mackerel with herbs*, cooked over a fire or in an oven. Today, we will make such fish at home — bake it in the oven with aromatic dried herbs, just like they did in taverns along the British coast. Get ready: tender fish, fragrant herbs, and a bit of culinary magic await you!

2. **What you need from the pirate's hold:**

— 1 fillet of cod or mackerel (or a whole fish, cleaned)
— 1 teaspoon of olive or sunflower oil
— ½ teaspoon of dried thyme
— ½ teaspoon of dried basil or oregano
— a pinch of salt
— a bit of black pepper
— a slice of lemon (optional)
— foil or a baking dish

3. **Preparing the fish — a privateer's care before the journey into the fire!**

If the fish is whole — ask an adult to clean it, remove the insides, gills, and head. If it's already a fillet — just rinse and pat dry with a paper towel. The fish should be dry — to absorb the aroma of the herbs well, like a sail catching the wind!

4. **Pirate marinade — the power in herbs!**

In a small bowl, mix the oil, thyme, basil, salt, and pepper. Rub this mixture all over the fish. If it's a fillet — just coat the top. If it's a whole fish — don't forget to rub inside the belly too! Let it stand for 10 minutes — let it soak up the flavor, like a sail catching the wind!

5. **Preparing for the journey into the oven!**

Place the fish on foil or in a baking dish. You can put a few slices of lemon on top — this will add aroma and freshness. Wrap in foil (if you want tender juicy fish) or leave open (for a golden crust).

6. **Baking — like releasing a ship into the voyage!**

Place in a preheated oven (180°C). Fillet bakes for 15–20 minutes. Whole fish — up to 25 minutes. If you're unsure if it's ready — ask an adult to check: the meat should easily separate with a fork and be white inside.

7. **Serving — like a feast on the captain's deck!**

Place the fish on a plate, garnish with greens, serve with mashed potatoes, rice, or just bread. Want to make it even more interesting — add a spoonful of sour cream or yogurt on top, as they did in port taverns!

8. **Tips from the privateer's galley:**

— Cod is soft and tender, while mackerel is fattier and more fragrant. Choose what you like more!
— If you want fish with a crispy crust — don't cover it completely with foil.
— You can add dried mint, lemon zest, or a bit of mustard — for a privateer's spicy character!

9. **Warning from the safety officer:**

The oven is hot, like a gun deck during battle! Don't touch it yourself — everything related to fire, we do *together with an adult*! Also, don't place foil directly on the oven rack — better on a baking sheet or in a dish.

10. **The fish is ready — a delicious stopover between sea exploits!**

When you taste the first piece — you will feel the aroma of herbs, the tenderness of the fish, and the warmth of baking. This is not just dinner — it's a real privateer's trophy after a long day of sails and waves. Eat slowly, savor — and remember: even simple fish with herbs can become a *legend of taste!*

Baked cod or mackerel with herbs — a pirate dinner with the aroma of the bay!

This dish is simple but noble — enjoyed by both simple sailors and the captain himself, sitting by the fire on the shore. Now you know how to cook it — and you can pass the recipe to the next generation of sea cooks! Bon appétit, privateer!

Apple Pudding: A Sweet Legend from the Privateer's Feast!

1. Hey, young pirate! It's time for a sweet dish that even the sternest privateers loved!

After the storm, sails, and adventures, everyone wants a bit of sweetness — and that's why *apple pudding* came to be. It contains the spirit of English gardens, a bit of pirate imagination, and a sea of flavor. It's not a complicated dessert, but it requires attention, warmth, and a spoonful of imagination. Gather all the ingredients — and set sail on a culinary boarding!

2. What you need — treasures from the galley hold:

— 2 medium apples (preferably sweet and sour)
— 1 egg
— 2 tablespoons of sugar
— 3 tablespoons of flour
— ½ teaspoon of baking powder
— 3 tablespoons of milk
— 1 teaspoon of butter
— a pinch of cinnamon (optional)
— a baking dish or a deep ceramic bowl

3. Let's start with the apples — juicy residents of English gardens.

Peel the apples (you can leave the skin if you prefer). Cut into cubes or thin slices. If you like soft pieces, stew the apples with a teaspoon of water and a pinch of sugar for 3–4 minutes in a pan (an adult can help). This will be the sweet base of our pudding.

4. Making the batter — soft as a sail in calm weather.

In a bowl, beat the egg with sugar using a whisk or fork. Add milk and mix. Then add flour with baking powder to make the batter slightly thick but flowing — like pirate sauce! Add melted butter and a bit of cinnamon for aroma. This is the pudding base that will gently envelop the apples.

5. Combining the treasures — apples and batter in one form.

Grease the form with butter. Place the apples at the bottom. Pour the batter on top. It will spread a bit and cover the fruit like a light spicy mist over the sea. If you like, sprinkle a bit more sugar on top for a crispy crust.

6. The oven — a pirate's cauldron! Let's bake.

With an adult, place the form in the oven preheated to 180°C. Bake for 20–25 minutes until golden brown. The pudding is ready when a toothpick or knife comes out clean, without batter. The aroma in the house is like a feast in a Cornish harbor!

7. Serving — on a plate with the mood of a captain's treat!

Let the pudding cool a bit (5–10 minutes) because a hot dessert is like a hot ship! Then cut into pieces or eat with a spoon straight from the dish. Serve with a spoonful of yogurt, jam, or even a scoop of ice cream if the ship is equipped with a freezer :)

8. Culinary tricks of the privateers:

— Instead of apples, you can use pears, plums, or berries.
— Want a very soft pudding? Add another spoonful of milk.
— If you have raisins, add them to the batter for a festive touch!
— And if you want to surprise, you can make a "cross" from the batter on top, like a real treasure map!

9. Warnings from the galley boatswain:

The oven is a hot zone. All manipulations with it are performed only by an adult! Also, be careful when working with a knife or hot form. And don't lick the spoon with raw batter, as the egg is not cooked yet!

10. Apple pudding — a gentle finale after the storm!

It's not just a dessert, but a story in every spoonful. Warm, soft, with the aroma of childhood and adventure. Such treats could be served in the captain's cabin after a victorious raid — when the ship is anchored, and the sea has finally calmed down.

Apple pudding — a sweet treasure worth seeking!

Now you know that even the simplest ingredients can become a magical dish if you add a bit of magical hands, warmth, and imagination. Enjoy, pirate, and remember: in every spoonful of pudding, there's a dream of new journeys!

Galette Biscuits: Crunchy Provisions for English Privateers!

1. Yo-ho-ho, young privateer! It's time to prepare biscuits that fear neither storm nor time!

Today we will prepare *galette biscuits* — hard, crunchy, and long-lasting, like a chest of gold. They were taken by *English pirates and privateers* on sea voyages because they don't spoil, don't crumble into dust, and won't make you seasick even in a storm. They are easy to make, but require a bit of patience — like standing watch!

2. Ingredients for the biscuits — like dry provisions from a frigate's hold:

— 1 cup of *flour (wheat or rye)*
— ¼ cup of *water*
— ½ tsp of *salt*
— 1 tbsp of *oil or melted butter*
— optional: a pinch of *herbs (thyme, rosemary)* or a pinch of *sugar*

3. Kneading the dough — like tightening ropes on the deck.

Pour the flour into a bowl, add salt, and mix. Gradually add water, kneading with a spoon or hands. Add the oil. The dough should become elastic, slightly firm, and not sticky. This is not a sweet biscuit — this is real *sea bread*!

4. **Rolling out — like unfolding a treasure map.**

Sprinkle the table with a little flour and roll out the dough *thinly — 3-5 mm*. Cut out circles (you can use a glass), squares, or simply make flatbreads. Poke each biscuit with a *fork* in several places — this is "drainage" to prevent it from puffing up like a sail in a storm!

5. **Baking — the galley is working at full capacity!**

Place the biscuits on a baking sheet (you can use parchment), ask an adult, and put them in a *preheated oven at 180°C* for *15–20 minutes* until they become hard and slightly golden. Don't overbake — galettes should be light but crunchy, like the side of a ship!

6. **Cooling time — as important as rest after a watch.**

Let the biscuits cool completely. While they are hot, they are still soft, but then they become strong, like a pirate's jacket! Store in an airtight tin or cloth bag — *like provisions for a long voyage*.

7. **Serving — on a privateer's table or under sail.**

Eat the galettes with *cheese, fish paste, honey, herbal grog*, or simply with tea. Pirates on board had lemon decoction — it went well with the biscuits. Also, *galettes can be crumbled into soup or broth* — it will be hearty and warming!

8. **Secrets from the old boatswain:**

— The *thinner* the dough, the *crunchier* the galettes.
— You can add a bit of honey — and it will be a "sweet privateer version."
— Want to make a "pirate snack"? Sprinkle with coarse salt or dried thyme on top!
— Keeps well for *up to 2 weeks*, and in an airtight container — even longer.

9. **Warnings from the ship's baker:**

— Don't use the oven without an adult.
— Don't touch hot biscuits with your hands — let them cool first!
— The dough is firm, but use a knife carefully.
— Don't eat too many at once — this is *expedition food*, not a cake!

10. Sea advice at the end of the culinary raid:

Galette biscuits are *traveler's food*, a *symbol of endurance and preparation*. They were taken on expeditions, hidden in chests, eaten in storms and calm. When you crunch on such a biscuit — you're not just eating, you're becoming part of ancient English maritime history. And that's true culinary magic!

Bon appétit, young privateer! May your galettes be crunchy, your bag full, and your adventures incredible. Until the next recipe from the *Pirate's Kitchen* — surely with new flavors, maps, and stormy stories!

Norwegian Vikings

1. Breakfast under the stars: dried cod and rye bread.

Norwegian Vikings started their day early — when the mist still hung over the fjords. They had a simple but hearty breakfast. Dried cod or salmon were the main protein heroes. They were served with dense rye bread, sometimes with butter or goat cheese. All of this was washed down with a fermented milk drink or a hot herbal brew of juniper or mint. Such a breakfast charged them for the whole day — whether on a boat or on the battlefield!

2. Sea soup: fish soup with barley.

For lunch, the Vikings prepared a hot soup — a true "fiskesuppe." It was a rich broth with sea fish (often cod or mackerel), vegetables (carrots, onions, parsnips), and grains — most often barley. It was cooked in a large cauldron over the fire, and dried seaweed was often added for flavor and salt. This soup was a warm shield against the cold northern wind.

3. Main dish: salmon on a willow skewer.

For dinner, Vikings loved to prepare fresh salmon skewered on a wooden willow skewer. The fish was roasted over an open fire, seasoned only with salt, wild dill, and sometimes juniper. The salmon was served with stewed cabbage or turnips. This was a festive meal — it was cooked in a large cauldron or simply over the fire, where the whole family or Viking crew gathered.

4. Side dishes from the fjords: porridge, cabbage, roots.

The favorite side dish was "grøt" — thick barley porridge with milk or just water. They also often ate stewed or fermented cabbage, carrots, turnips, and parsnips. These vegetables stored well in cellars and were available year-round. The side dishes were not flashy, but they created a warm, hearty contrast to the fish.

5. Snacks for the road: dried salmon.

On a journey, Vikings took dried or cured salmon, which could last for weeks. Another popular snack was a fermented fish product, which had a strong smell but was nutritious and beneficial. They ate it with bread or simply chewed pieces — like pirate chips! It was energy in the pocket.

6. Beverages: mead and barley infusion.

Vikings knew their drinks! The most famous was "mjød" — a drink made from honey, water, and wild herbs, which could be either light or festive. On weekdays, they more often drank barley infusion — a weak grain drink that replaced water. They also consumed sour milk or whey, especially children. Water was not always clean, so herbal or grain drinks saved the crew's health.

7. Desserts from the north: honey nuts and cheese mass.

For dessert, Vikings enjoyed nuts in honey, if they managed to get hazelnuts or acorns. They also made cheese mass from goat's milk and sweetened it with honey or berries. Berries — blackberries, cloudberries, blueberries — were collected in summer and dried or stored in clay pots. Even in the harshest winter, one could enjoy something sweet, like a true jarl!

8. **Communal dinner in the "longhouse" — tradition and ritual.**

Vikings dined together in the "longhouse" — a large wooden hall with a hearth in the middle. Food was laid out on long tables, and everyone had a wooden bowl and spoon. After the meal — songs, tales, sometimes stories about Odin and sea monsters. The communal meal was not just about food — it was part of the soul of their people.

9. **Provisions for the boat: barrels, bags, and dried salmon.**

On the ship, Vikings took food in barrels and bags: dried fish, grain, fermented cabbage, cheese, and honey. In special "butter churns" — fatty fish oil, which could be used to dress porridge. The food had to be light, long-lasting, and energy-giving. It was their northern ration — simple but with character.

10. **Viking cuisine — strength, taste, and spirit of the northern sea.**

Vikings ate simply but powerfully. Fish, grains, vegetables, milk, and honey created a menu that helped them travel, fight, trade, and discover new lands. Each dish was not just sustenance but part of the legend they left in history. And it was proof that even the fiercest warriors know how to cook deliciously and with soul.

The cuisine of Norwegian Vikings is a culinary saga: about fish that smells of the sea; about porridge that warms the chest; about honey that gives strength. It teaches: in simplicity lies true strength. And even in cold Norway, among icebergs and waves, food can be a warm hearth for all who believe in the team and adventures.

Fiskesuppe with sour cream: Norwegian fish soup for a young Viking!

1. **Emerald fjords are calling — let's cook fish soup!**

Welcome, little Viking! Today we will prepare a dish that your distant sea ancestors ate after windy voyages — *fiskesuppe*, a warm fish soup with vegetables, herbs, and... sour cream! Yes, instead of cream, we will use sour cream — it will add a bit of tang, like a breeze from the northern sea. And don't forget, young captain: always work with an adult helper in the galley!

2. **Gathering ingredients — like a Viking gathering provisions in the port.**

You will need:
— 300 g of white fish fillet (cod, hake, or pike-perch)
— 1 carrot
— 1 onion
— 1 small potato
— 1 celery root or a piece of parsnip
— 1 liter of water or fish broth
— 3 tablespoons of sour cream (15-20%)
— 1 bay leaf
— a bit of butter or oil
— salt, pepper
— herbs — dill or parsley

3. **Fish on board!**

Thoroughly rinse the fillet, make sure there are no bones (this is a task for an adult!). Cut the fish into small pieces — like little icebergs floating in the soup.

4. **Vegetables — colorful cargo for the soup.**

Carrot, potato, celery, and onion — all set off on a journey together! Cut everything neatly into cubes or slices. Be careful, the knife is like a Viking's sword, but for vegetables!

5. **Sautéing — the smell of a northern fire.**

Melt a bit of butter in a pan or pot. First, add the onion — it will "call" other flavors, like a Viking horn. Add the carrot and celery, sauté for a few minutes until the vegetables become softer and fragrant.

6. **Water — the sea in a pot!**

Pour everything with water or broth, add the potato and bay leaf. Cook for 10-12 minutes on low heat. Our boat sails smoothly, without a storm — make sure the soup doesn't boil over!

7. **Fish docking!**

Add the fish carefully, so it doesn't fall apart. Cook for another 5-7 minutes. It should be soft and tender, like a Scandinavian siren's song.

8. **Sour cream magic — white mist over the fjord.**

Reduce the heat. In a small bowl, mix 3 tablespoons of sour cream with a few tablespoons of hot soup (this is called "tempering" to prevent the sour cream from curdling). Then pour the mixture into the pot and gently stir. The soup will become soft, slightly tangy — perfect for a Viking chilled on the deck!

9. **Captain's garnish.**

Chop the herbs (dill, parsley, or even green onion) and add to the soup. You can top it with a spoonful of fresh sour cream — it will look like an iceberg in a sea of flavor! It's best served with bread or Scandinavian croutons.

10. **Useful tips from the north:**

— Do not let the sour cream boil — it may curdle.
— For a richer flavor, you can add a bit of lemon juice — but only a few drops.
— If you want to add fish accents — add a bit of smoked fish or shrimp (but this is for older captains!).
— Always keep an eye on the stove — a true Viking never leaves the ship unattended!

And here it is — warm, tender fiskesuppe with sour cream!

This dish embraces you like a fur cloak after a cold raid. Let this aromatic soup warm you, young Viking, and inspire you for new delicious adventures. Heia Norge!

Klippfisk: dried cod for true sea vikings!

1. **Greetings, young viking! Let's prepare to dry cod the Norwegian way!**

Today we will make a true dish of Norwegian seafarers — *klippfisk* (dried cod on the rocks). Long ago, vikings, much like pirates, took this fish on long journeys. Why? It keeps well, is light, and tastes great after boiling. But drying fish is like creating your own little food treasure. Let's start this northern adventure!

2. **What is klippfisk and why is it important for vikings?**

Klippfisk is cod that is first salted and then dried in the air or in a well-ventilated place. The name comes from the word "klippe" (rock) — because the fish was placed directly on stones on the coast. For you at home, this could be a balcony, attic, or a net on a stand.

3. **Treasure ingredients for the viking project.**

Here's what you need:
— fresh cod fillet (preferably thick pieces, boneless)
— coarse salt (can be sea salt)
— cheesecloth or fly net
— flat tray or wooden rack
— a place with good air (for example, a balcony or loggia)

4. **Salting the cod — like a true sea master.**

First, you need to salt the fish. This will make it safe for storage and tasty. For each piece of fish, sprinkle a lot of salt — enough to cover it on all sides. Layer the fish in a bowl: a layer of fish, a layer of salt, fish again. Place the bowl in the refrigerator or in a cool place for *2 days*.

5. **Rinsing and preparing for drying.**

After 2 days, remove the fish from the salt and rinse well under cold water to remove the excess. Then pat it dry with a towel. Now it's ready for the big journey — drying!

6. Choosing a place — vikings dried on rocks, you — on the balcony.

Place the pieces of cod on a rack or tray with holes to allow air to pass underneath. Cover with cheesecloth or netting to protect from flies. It's important that the place is dry, ventilated, and *not in direct sunlight*, as the fish will become as tough as a sword!

7. Patient captain — the fish dries slowly.

Drying can take from *5 to 10 days*, depending on the weather. Turn the fish daily to ensure it dries evenly. If it rains outside, move it indoors with ventilation. Remember: patience is the main weapon of a viking cook!

8. Signs of readiness — how to know the fish is now klippfisk.

The fish should become dry, but not like a stone. It should be firm, slightly flexible, like leather armor. The smell should be pleasant, salty. If everything is like this — then you are a true drying hero of the North!

9. Storage — how to store your dried catch.

When the fish is dry, place it in a paper bag or box. Do not keep it in plastic — it may "suffocate." In a dry place, it can be stored for *up to a year*. Before cooking, it should be *soaked overnight in water*. Then you can make soup, stew, fry — whatever your viking soul desires!

10. Tips and warnings from wise vikings.

— Always work with clean hands!
— The fish should be well rinsed after salting — otherwise, it will be too salty.
— Protect it from insects with cheesecloth.
— If you have a cat — do not leave the fish unattended!
— Ensure there is no moisture — otherwise, the fish may spoil.

That's it, young viking!

Now you know how to make klippfisk — a true dish of Norwegian seafarers. It accompanied them in cold seas, on long journeys, and even at festive feasts in longhouses. It's more than just food — it's a part of culture and endurance. And who knows — maybe one day your klippfisk will embark on a journey with you!

Hot-Smoked Salmon: The Aromatic Fish of the Vikings!

1. Greetings, young Viking! Today we smoke fish like the ancient sea heroes!

In the northern lands, among the fjords and frosty winds, Norwegian Vikings prepared food that lasted long and had a magical smoky aroma. Hot-smoked salmon is one of those dishes. Today, you will learn to prepare this legendary fish with an adult, because smoking is a serious business! Prepare your apron, a brave heart, and a nose ready for smoky adventures!

2. What is hot smoking and why did the Vikings love it?

Hot smoking is when fish is cooked in smoke at a high temperature (from 60 to 80°C). Unlike cold smoking, it is ready to eat immediately! It was the perfect way for Vikings to make food tasty, aromatic, and long-lasting. Plus, Vikings adored smoke because it smelled like a real expedition!

3. Ingredients from the fjords for a great smoking battle.

Needed:
— 1 piece of salmon fillet (can be with skin)
— coarse sea salt
— a bit of sugar
— pepper (optional)
— a little lemon juice (or lime for a tropical pirate mood)
— wood chips or shavings (beech, alder, apple — *not coniferous!*)
— smoker or grill with a lid

4. Salting the fish — an ancient Viking preservation ritual.

Place the salmon on a board. Mix salt and a bit of sugar (3 tablespoons of salt to 1 tablespoon of sugar). Sprinkle the fish with this mixture on both sides and place it in a container. Leave in the refrigerator for 2–3 hours. This will make it juicy and aromatic.

5. Rinsing and drying — preparing the fish for smoke!

Take out the fish, rinse it under cold water to wash off the salt. Pat dry with a paper towel. Then place it on a rack to dry for 30–60 minutes

The surface will become slightly sticky — this is perfect for smoke. This is called *pellicle*, and it helps the smoke "stick" to the fish!

6. Preparing the smoker — fire, smoke, and a bit of magic!

Ask an adult to help with the smoker. Sprinkle chips at the bottom, place a drip tray, a rack — and on it, the fish skin-side down. Turn on the heat. If it's a grill — place the chips in foil with holes. The temperature inside should be about 70°C. Hot, but not blazing!

7. Smoking — patiently, like a true sailor in a storm.

Smoking lasts *30–60 minutes*, depending on the thickness of the fish. Check from time to time if there is smoke and if the heat is not too strong. Do not open the lid too often — the smoke should stay inside, like magic in a Viking forge!

8. How to know when the salmon is ready?

The meat should become pink-orange, juicy, but easily separate with a fork. If you have a kitchen thermometer, the center of the fish should be *at least 60°C*. And it smells just incredible: like forest, sea, and a bit of adventure!

9. Serving the salmon — like at a northern feast.

Serve the smoked salmon with rye bread, boiled potatoes, greens, or just a drop of lemon juice. Vikings loved to eat with their hands — so serve without unnecessary knives and forks! Want even more pirate charm? Wrap it in parchment, like a treasure scroll!

10. Secrets and warnings from the culinary skald.

— Always smoke *outdoors or on a balcony* — smoke is not for kitchens!
— Never leave the fire unattended. Fire is a friend, but unpredictable!
— Do not use pine or painted chips — they are toxic.
— Smoke only with an adult! It's like swimming in the sea — not worth it alone.
— Don't rush — aromatic food is born slowly!

Congratulations, young Viking!

Now you know how to prepare real smoked salmon — a dish enjoyed by the warriors of Scandinavia after a battle or a long journey. Feel the smoke, listen to the crackle of wood, and remember: every piece carries the spirit of adventure, strength, and tradition. *Bon appétit, and may the smoke always rise, and the sword stay down!*

Salmon on a Skewer: A Fiery Dish of the Northern Vikings!

1. Hello, young Viking! Today we are cooking fish over the fire — like the ancient sea heroes!

Vikings didn't have microwaves or stoves — they cooked right over the flames, under the open sky. Salmon on a skewer was one of their favorite dishes: simple, hearty, and delicious. We will recreate this magic, just don't forget — work together with an adult! Because real fire, like the sea, does not forgive carelessness!

2. What do we need for a culinary fiery raid?

Here's your list of provisions:
— fresh boneless salmon fillet (can be with skin)
— salt, pepper, lemon (or lime — for a tropical pirate mood)
— a bit of honey or olive oil
— wooden or metal skewers
— a bonfire or grill (only outdoors!)
— foil (optional)

3. Cutting the salmon — like a skilled axeman from the fjord.

Cut the salmon fillet into pieces of 4–5 cm — not too thin, so they don't fall apart. If you're working with a knife — definitely with an adult! Vikings valued fish not only as food but also as a catch, so treat it with respect.

4. Salting and marinating — adding the spirit of northern herbs.

Salt the fish, add a bit of pepper. Mix 1 tablespoon of olive oil with a few drops of lemon juice and a bit of honey — this will make the fish aromatic and golden when frying. Let it marinate for 20–30 minutes. In the meantime — light the bonfire with an adult helper!

5. Skewers at the ready — the weapon of a culinary Viking.

Thread the salmon pieces onto the skewers. If using wooden ones — soak them in water for 30 minutes so they don't burn. Thread carefully so the pieces don't slip into the fire — because even Vikings felt regret when fish fell into the bonfire!

6. Lighting the bonfire — how to do it without a drakkar.

Stack the wood with an adult in the shape of a "hut" or "well." Light the bonfire and wait until the fire subsides a bit and embers appear. Embers are the gold for frying, as direct flames are too wild! It's better to grill not over the flames, but over the smoldering fire.

7. Grilling — like at a feast after a victory over the storm.

Hold the skewer over the embers (not over the flames!) and carefully turn every 1–2 minutes. Salmon cooks quickly — 8–12 minutes. It should become pink inside and slightly crispy on the outside. Don't overcook it, because even Vikings didn't like dry fish!

8. Want it even cooler? Wrap the fish in foil!

If you're afraid the fish will fall or dry out, wrap the pieces in foil along with herbs, a slice of lemon, and a spoonful of butter. Grill on the embers right in the wrap — it will be tender and very juicy. Vikings may not have had foil, but we are modern warriors of fire!

9. Serving — like at a feast in a hall with horned helmets!

Serve the salmon right on the skewer or remove it onto a wooden board. Add boiled potatoes, rye bread, or a piece of cucumber. You can garnish with herbs, like a true culinary jarl. And don't forget — grilled fish tastes best by the bonfire under the birds' songs and the waves' splash.

10. **Warnings and tips from the fiery skald.**

— Always cook with an adult — fire is not a toy!
— Don't touch the skewer with your hands right after grilling — it's hot!
— Watch the fish so it doesn't burn.
— Don't leave the bonfire unattended — even Vikings didn't burn their camps!
— Cooking is not a race. Calmness is the weapon of a true fiery cook.
Bon appétit, young Viking by the fire!

Now you know how to cook salmon like the warriors on the northern coast did before setting out on their journeys. Salmon, a bonfire, and the power of nature — that's all you need for an unforgettable meal. May your skewer always be full, and the fire gentle and strong!

Stewed Herring with Turnip and Roots: An Ancient Viking Dish!

1. **Scandinavian greetings, young Viking! Today — culinary from the past!**

We embark on a true culinary journey to the times when Vikings hadn't heard of potatoes yet. But no worries! They had other delicious treasures: *turnip, parsnip, celery root, wild onion, and sauerkraut.* Today we will prepare stewed herring just as they did — without potatoes, but with the spirit of the fjords!

2. **Ingredients — the generosity of the northern land and sea.**

Here's what we need:
— 2 salted herrings (or fillets)
— 1–2 turnips
— 1 parsnip
— 1 small celery root
— half a cup of sauerkraut
— 1 onion or wild onion (or green onion)
— bay leaf, peppercorns
— water
— a bit of butter or lard (can use butter fat)

3. **Herring — the main star of the northern pot.**

Salted herring should be soaked in cold water for 1–2 hours. This will help reduce the salt and make the taste milder. If the herring is whole, ask an adult to clean and fillet it. Vikings had their own knives for this, but you should use a safe option — with help!

4. **Root vegetables — northern strength instead of potatoes.**

Peel the turnip, parsnip, and celery root. Cut them into cubes or slices — however is convenient (and safe) for you. Ask an adult to help with the hard vegetables — they are as tough as a Viking's beard! Slice the onion into half rings.

5. **Start cooking — place the fish into the vegetable boat.**

Melt a bit of butter in a deep pan or pot. Sauté the onion until translucent — it will give a sweet aroma. Then layer: turnip, celery, parsnip, sauerkraut, and herring fillet. Add a bay leaf and a few peppercorns.

6. **Add water and stew — not quickly, but calmly like the sea.**

Pour in water to barely cover the vegetables. Cover with a lid. Stew *on low heat for 30–40 minutes* until all the vegetables are soft and the flavors meld. Don't forget to keep an eye on it and occasionally stir with a wooden spoon — just like on a ship's kitchen!

7. **The spirit of the fjords — how does a real Viking dish smell?**

Stewed turnip, parsnip, and celery smell sweet, but with a slight tang from the sauerkraut and the saltiness of the fish — this is the true aroma of the north. If you close your eyes — imagine a Viking wooden hall, where the fire roars and the sound of swords on the walls is heard.

8. **Serving — like at a Viking feast after battle.**

Place the vegetables on a wooden plate with the fish on top. If you wish, you can add a spoonful of butter or a piece of black bread on the side. Eat with a spoon, sitting straight, as the warriors did on the shore after landing. Just don't throw food — even Vikings had etiquette!

9. **Secrets of ancient cooks.**

— Add sauerkraut carefully — it adds tang but shouldn't overpower the taste.
— If the fish is very salty — soak longer or change the water several times.
— Stewing is about patience. The slower, the tastier.
— If there's no parsnip — you can substitute with carrot (but it's later, not always available in those times).

10. **Caution from the kitchen skald.**

— Never cut vegetables on your own if you haven't yet mastered holding a knife well.
— Don't open the lid yourself — the steam is hot!
— If the dish seems unusual to you — give it a chance: you're tasting history!
— Be careful with pepper and bay leaf — they add aroma, but you don't need much.

Bon appétit, young warrior of the north!

Now you know how to prepare real *Scandinavian stewed fish*, enjoyed even before the discovery of America! This dish warmed hearts, gave strength, and united the sea with the land on one plate. Eat slowly, think of distant voyages — and prepare for the next culinary saga!

Sea Soup with Turnip: A Viking Soup for the Brave!

1. Hello, young sailor! It's time to cook a real soup with the spirit of the sea!

In the north, where cold winds blow through the fjords and Viking ships sail the waves, hot soup saves from cold and fatigue. Today we will prepare *sea soup with turnip* — a dish Vikings enjoyed after a battle or a long journey. We will cook together with an adult, as this dish involves fire, a knife, and water!

2. **Scandinavian Basket: Ingredients from the Sea and Land.**

We need:
— 1–2 fillets of sea fish (for example, cod or herring)
— 1–2 turnips
— 1 carrot
— 1 small onion or green onion
— a few black peppercorns
— bay leaf
— greens (nettle, wild parsley, or something similar)
— water
— salt

3. **Preparing the Fish — Like a Treasure Caught from the Northern Sea.**

The fish needs to be washed, and if it's whole, carefully separate the fillet (an adult does this). If you already have fillet — great! Check for any bones. Vikings didn't like surprises in their soup!

4. **Peeling Vegetables — Northern Turnip Instead of Exotic.**

Peel the turnip, carrot, and onion. Cut the turnip into cubes, the carrot into circles, and the onion as you like (you can even leave it whole for flavor and then remove it). These are simple vegetables that grew in the rocky soil of Norway — real strength for the soup!

5. **Put the Pot on the Fire — The Culinary Adventure Begins!**

Pour water into a pot — about 1 liter. Add the bay leaf, a few peppercorns, and all the vegetables. Put it on the stove and turn on the heat. When the water boils, reduce the heat and cook for 15 minutes. Don't leave the stove unattended — a true captain keeps an eye on the course!

6. **Adding the Fish — A Wave of Flavor Rolls Through the Soup.**

When the vegetables are almost soft, add the fish to the pot. Cook for another 10 minutes — the fish cooks quickly. It should become white and easily separate with a fork. Don't stir too much — Vikings valued whole pieces of fish!

7. **Add Some Greens — In Honor of the Fjord's Nature.**

At the very end, add a pinch of greens — nettle, wild parsley, or whatever you have on hand. The greens will add aroma, like a spring wind over the fjord. Salt to taste (if the fish wasn't salty), but be careful — the sea already brings salt!

8. **How to Know the Soup is Ready?**

The vegetables are soft, the fish is tender, the aroma is like after a storm: fresh and strong. Taste a spoonful (careful — it's hot!). If it's tasty and warm — you've succeeded as a true culinary jarl.

9. **Serving — Like at a Viking Feast After a Sea Battle.**

Pour the soup into a clay or wooden bowl. You can eat with a wooden spoon or drink directly from the bowl — as the warriors did by the fire. Add a slice of black bread on the side — and you have a meal worthy of a drakkar!

10. **Tips and Precautions from the Soup Captain.**

— Always wash your hands before starting.
— Don't touch the hot pot by yourself.
— Don't leave the stove unattended!
— If using a whole fish — be sure to remove the bones.
— The taste of the soup is better revealed if you let it stand for 10 minutes under the lid after cooking.

Bon appétit, little Viking!

Now you know how to cook *sea soup with turnip*, just like the warriors on the shores of Scandinavia did many centuries ago. In every spoonful — the breath of the northern sea, the warmth of the fire, and the strength of simple gifts of nature. Eat with pride — and prepare for new culinary sagas!

Rye Flatbreads with Fish Paste: A Viking Snack for Sea Adventures!

1. **Hello, young pirate from the north! Let's prepare for a fish-flatbread expedition!**

Today we will make *rye flatbreads with fish paste* — a simple, hearty, and delicious dish that Vikings took with them on sea voyages. The flatbreads are like ship shields, and the paste is like a gift from the sea. This snack kept the warriors strong in battle, and us — on the kitchen front. So put on your apron — and let's cook together with an adult!

2. **Ingredients — gifts of the land and sea.**

For the rye flatbreads:
— 1 cup rye flour
— ½ cup warm water
— a pinch of salt
— 1 tablespoon oil (or melted fat)

For the fish paste:
— 1 fillet of boiled or smoked fish (cod, mackerel, herring)
— 1 tablespoon butter (or oil)
— a bit of chopped onion or greens
— a pinch of salt, lemon juice (optional)

3. **Flatbreads — the warrior's bread, strong as his sword.**

In a bowl, pour in the rye flour, salt, and add water. Stir with a spoon, then with your hands. The dough should be soft, not sticky. If needed, add a bit more flour. This is a job for a strong sailor (or an adult helper). Then set the dough aside for 10 minutes — let it rest, like a ship before setting sail.

4. **Rolling and frying — like in a Viking camp.**

Divide the dough into 4 parts. Roll each into a circle or simply shape it with your hands, like a flat stone. Fry on a dry pan or with a drop of oil — 2–3 minutes on each side. They should become golden and firm — like shields on the deck of a drakkar!

5. **Fish paste — a tasty trophy from a sea journey.**

Mash the boiled or smoked fish with a fork. Add butter, onion, a pinch of salt, and a few drops of lemon. Mix everything well. If the paste is dry, add a bit more butter or a drop of warm water. You can mix it with your hands too — Vikings weren't afraid to get messy!

6. **Secrets from the kitchen captain.**

— Smoked fish is best for the paste — aromatic, like a mountain campfire.
— If using boiled fish, add a bit of salt and butter for flavor.
— Instead of butter, you can use grated egg or homemade cheese.
— You can make the flatbreads thinner if you like — they'll become crispy!

7. **Combining forces — flatbread + paste = a victorious dish!**

Spread some fish paste on the ready flatbread. You can roll it up or fold it in half, like a sea envelope. Eat it warm or wrap it in parchment and take it on a journey — like a true Viking setting sail!

8. **Serving — like at a northern feast under the stars.**

Place the flatbreads on a wooden board, garnish with a few sprigs of greens (like dill) and drops of lemon juice. You can serve it with a honey drink or milk. And if you have a cauldron on the fire — add some hot soup to them!

9. **Warnings from the shore cook.**

— Don't work with a hot pan alone — call an adult helper!
— Check the fish for bones before using.
— Is the dough sticky? Add a bit of flour, but don't overdo it — otherwise, it will become tough.
— Add butter or fat gradually — don't drown the paste, or it will "sail off the board."

10. **Useful advice from the skald-chef:**

Rye flatbreads with fish paste are not just food, but a part of history. When you make them, you repeat the actions of those who lived a thousand years ago: catching fish, baking bread on stone, and setting off on journeys without fear. And now — you are one of them!

Enjoy, young Viking with a spoon and the heart of a brave sailor!

Now you have your own *Viking snack* — hearty, simple, and delicious. Such food fears neither time, rain, nor waves. Eat, dream, and prepare for new culinary adventures — many more dishes from the Pirate's Kitchen await!

Tartar from Salted Salmon: A Cold Dish with the Hot Spirit of the North!

1. Hello, little Viking chef! Today's dish is without fire, but with the fire of flavor!

In this culinary journey, we will prepare *tartar from salted salmon* — a cold but very tasty appetizer that Vikings could eat from delicate pieces of sea bounty. Tartar is a dish without thermal processing, so it is prepared quickly but requires attention, cleanliness, and fresh ingredients. And, of course, an adult on board!

2. What is tartar and why could Vikings love it?

Tartar is finely chopped raw or salted fish with additives: greens, onions, spices. Vikings didn't have blenders, but they had knives, salt, and smoke. They salted salmon, stored it in barrels, and then ate it with bread, turnips, or just with a spoon — just like we will prepare now!

3. Ingredients — treasures from the sea and the green shore.

Here's what you need:
— 100–150 g *salted salmon* (fillet, boneless)
— 1 tsp olive oil (or a drop of flaxseed oil)
— 1 tsp chopped green onion or wild leek
— a bit of dill or parsley
— a few drops of lemon juice
— black pepper (carefully!)
— optionally — grated boiled egg or grated radish

4. Fish preparation — precision at the level of a sea navigator.

Take a piece of salted salmon (if it's very salty — rinse and soak it a bit). Check for bones. This is important! Then, carefully cut it into small cubes — the smaller, the better. This is done by an adult or you under supervision. Vikings also knew how to work with a knife, but always with respect!

5. Greens and additives — a gift from the fjord shore.

Finely chop the greens and onion. Mix everything in a bowl with the fish. Add a little oil and a drop of lemon juice — this will make the taste fresher, like the wind from the sea. If you want, you can add a spoonful of grated boiled egg or grated radish: this will add creaminess or spiciness.

6. Secrets from the northern chef.

— The best is *homemade salted fillet* — not too salty, without skin, and with good texture.
— If you don't like a very strong taste, add more greens — it balances the saltiness.
— Don't be afraid to experiment with additives: a bit of grated apple — and it will be even more interesting!

7. Form — make it like in the earl's banquet hall!

Take a small cup or round mold. Put the tartar in it and gently press with a spoon. Then turn it over onto a plate — it will make a beautiful tower, like a fortress on the shore. Or you can simply place it with a spoon on a piece of rye bread — simply and deliciously Viking-style!

8. Serving — as an appetizer before a sea adventure!

Garnish the dish with a few sprigs of greens, a few grains of boiled egg, or even a cranberry (yes, they grew in Norway!). Serve with bread, crispy bread, or just on a lettuce leaf. And be sure to say: *"For Odin!"* before tasting!

9. **Warnings from the kitchen galley guard.**

— The fish must be *fresh and properly salted* — don't cook with dubious ones.
— Don't leave it in the warmth for long — this is a dish to be eaten immediately.
— Work with a knife *only with an adult*!
— Don't add too much lemon — it can "overcook" the fish.
— If in doubt — it's better to make the fish boiled and then cut it.

10. **Historical advice from the skald.**

Vikings didn't always eat hot food — on the road, on board, or in ambush, they consumed what could be eaten quickly and without fire. Tartar from salted salmon is not only delicious but also *a part of the true culinary history of the north*. When you eat it, you feel a connection with the sea, the forest, and ancient traditions!

Bon appétit, brave chef of the northern seas!

Now your culinary diary has another dish — *tartar from salted salmon*, simple but noble, like sails on a drakkar. Cook boldly, eat with pleasure — and get ready for the next culinary saga of the Pirate Kitchen!

«Mjod»: a drink of strength and sun for young Vikings!

1. **Scandinavian greetings, young brewer! Today we will create a legendary drink!**

Real Vikings drank "mjod" — a drink based on honey, water, and wild herbs. Adults had their fermented mjod (like mead), but we will prepare a *non-alcoholic version* — tasty, aromatic, and healthy. It will be a sweet drink that could be served at a feast in the jarl's hall or on a drakkar after a victorious raid!

2. **Honey treasure list — what to gather on the kitchen shore?**

We will need:
— 1 liter of water
— 3-4 tablespoons of honey (preferably natural)
— a few sprigs of mint
— 1-2 sprigs of thyme or oregano
— a piece of lemon (or a few rosehip/cranberry berries)
— optionally — calendula petals, lemon balm leaves, dried elderflower or chamomile

3. Gathering and preparing herbs — treasures from the wild land.

Pick (or take dried) *aromatic and safe herbs*. If you gather them yourself — always with an adult and only what you know! The best are mint, thyme, lemon balm, chamomile flowers. Wash the herbs and let them dry a bit — they should be as clean as new armor before a campaign!

4. Boiling water — the source of warmth for our drink.

Ask an adult to boil 1 liter of water. When it boils, reduce the heat and *add the herbs to the water*. Simmer on low heat for *5-7 minutes* to let the aroma unfold like the sails of a ship. Then remove from heat and let it steep for *15-20 minutes* under a lid.

5. Straining — like filtering treasures from sand.

When the decoction cools a bit, strain it through a sieve or cheesecloth. You will have aromatic, warm herbal water. It smells of forests, meadows, and a bit of magic!

6. Adding honey — the sunlit gold of the Vikings.

Now, when the liquid is *warm but not hot* (it doesn't burn your finger!), add the honey. Hot water kills beneficial substances, so wait until the drink cools a bit. Stir with a spoon, like stirring the sea before a storm!

7. Cooling or serving warm — the captain decides.

The drink can be consumed *warm* if it's winter outside or you've just returned from a battle on a snowy field. Or you can cool it in a jug — and drink it cold in the heat, like after exertion with a shield and helmet!

8. Serving — like at a feast in a great hall with horned helmets.

Pour the mjod into a clay cup or wooden mug. Garnish with a mint leaf or flower petals. Place the jug in the center of the table — like Vikings at celebrations! And say: "*Glory to the drink!*" before taking the first sip.

9. Secrets and variations from the coastal healer.

— You can add *pieces of apple or pear* for a fruity taste.
— If you want an immune-boosting drink — add a bit of *grated ginger* or a few rosehip berries.
— You can bottle it and drink it the next day — the taste will only intensify.
— For color, add *a bit of cranberry or hibiscus* — like the blood of an enemy (jokingly, of course!).

10. Warnings from the wise kitchen guardian.

— Do not drink mjod hot — *honey loses its benefits at high temperatures*.
— Do not add too many herbs — the drink will be bitter.
— Do not drink too much at once — even a magical drink is better savored slowly.
— And most importantly — do not gather wild herbs yourself if you are not 100% sure about them!
Glory to the drink, young Viking!

Now you know how to prepare your first *mjod* — a drink of strength, warmth, and the taste of the north. In it — the honey apiaries of Scandinavia, the winds over the fjords, and the soul of true sea heroes. Drink with honor, treat your friends — and be ready for a new culinary adventure!

Goat Cheese with Dill and Herbs: A Cream for Viking Breads!

1. Greetings, young Viking! Today we create cheese as it was made in the highlands of Scandinavia!

Vikings didn't always eat fish or meat. In the mountains, they kept goats, milked them, and made *simple fermented cheese* — soft, slightly salty, with herbs and the aroma of wild nature. Today, we will prepare it at home: without large vats, but with great desire!

2. Gathering ingredients — like a green hunt!

We will need:
— 1 liter of *goat sour milk* (or sour kefir without additives)
— 2 cups of water
— 1 teaspoon of salt
— a few sprigs of *fresh or dried dill*
— a bit of *mint, nettle, oregano, or thyme* (can be dried)
— cheesecloth or a very clean towel
— a pot, colander, and bowl

3. Herbal magic — from the field to the pot.

Wash the dill and other herbs well. Chop finely — they will add not only flavor to the cheese but also appearance, like a mosaic of forest colors. If using dried herbs, simply rub them between your fingers. Vikings believed that the aroma of herbs protected against evil spirits... and added strength!

4. Heating the milk — carefully, like a wizard with a copper cauldron.

Pour the sour milk into a pot. Ask an adult to *turn on the stove* and heat the milk to a *hot but not boiling* state (about 60–70°C). When the milk starts to *curdle* and white lumps appear — it's a sign that the cheese is being born!

5. Adding herbs and salt — like a Viking to the cauldron before battle.

Add salt and herbs to the pot. Stir gently with a wooden spoon. Remove from heat and let it steep for 5 minutes — so the herbs "release their spirit." At this moment, it smells as if you are in a camp on a mountain edge!

6. **Straining — like separating treasures from sand.**

Place a colander over a bowl, line it with cheesecloth. Slowly pour the mixture. The whey (yellowish water) will drain down, and the cheese will remain in the cheesecloth. Be careful — it's hot! Let it drain for 10–15 minutes. Then gather the edges of the cheesecloth and gently press with a spoon or hands.

7. **Forming the cheese lump — a culinary trophy of the Viking.**

Leave the cheese in the cheesecloth for 30–40 minutes under a light press (for example, a jar of water). It will become denser but soft. This will not be a hard cheese, but a *spread or a delicate cheese ball*, like a creamy cloud from a mountain farm.

8. **Serving — on flatbreads, bread, leaves, or... a spoon!**

Serve the ready cheese on rye flatbreads, bread, or even just on a lettuce leaf. Garnish with a sprig of dill on top. Vikings spread it on wooden plates or ate it with a spoon, as we do today — to your health!

9. **Secrets from the northern cauldron:**

— The cheese is delicious both warm and chilled — store in the refrigerator for up to 3 days.
— Instead of goat milk, you can try cow's milk, but the aroma will be different.
— If you want thicker cheese — keep it under the press longer.
— Add a bit of honey instead of salt — and you'll get a sweet snack!

10. **Precautions from the cheese guardian:**

— Only an adult heats the milk — the pot is hot!
— Do not touch the cheesecloth while it's hot — let it cool.
— Do not use herbs you don't know — only trusted ones!
— If the milk doesn't curdle — add 1–2 tablespoons of lemon juice or a bit of sour kefir.

Bon appétit, young creator of the cheese saga!

Now you know how to make *goat cheese with herbs*, as shepherds and travelers of the fjords did.

It's not just a dish — it's an edible legend passed from campfire to campfire.
Enjoy it — and prepare for a new culinary journey of the Pirate's Kitchen!

Pirate Secrets: Tactics, Tricks, and a Little Magic from All the Seas!

1. Caribbean Pirates — Masters of Ambushes and Coconut Tricks.

Caribbean pirates are the same rascals we see in movies with treasures and
parrots. They loved to hide in coral coves, waiting for Spanish trading ships.
Their tactic was a lightning attack! They knew when the wind would blow, how
the currents worked, and even used overturned boats to hide at night. In
battle, they often used pepper smoke bombs to blind the enemy and board the
ship.

2. Barbary Pirates — The Terror of the Mediterranean from North Africa.

Pirates from the coasts of Tunisia, Algeria, and Morocco, known as Berber or
Barbary pirates, were not just bandits — they had real naval bases and even
treaties with sultans. Their tactic was quick raids at night. They attacked
European coastal cities and hunted ships, but also used disguises: their ships
often looked like trading vessels until it was too late. And they spoke several
languages fluently to negotiate or... deceive!

3. Somali Pirates — Modern Pirates with Ancient Techniques.

Although today Somali pirates are no longer the ancient pirate brothers, their
tactics have historical roots. Ancient Somali sailors attacked ships carrying
spices and gold. They knew every current of the Indian Ocean and used small
but fast boats. Modern pirates use radio communication, but sometimes act
just like their ancestors: quietly, precisely, and unexpectedly.

4. Malabar Pirates — Traders and Warriors from Kerala.

Malabar pirates from the southwest of India were very clever. They not only
robbed but also traded. Their favorite strategy was to let a ship anchor as if it
were safe, and then — attack! They knew the stars well and used them for
navigation. They also had agreements with local princes — "you give me
spices, I give you protection from other pirates."

5. South China Sea Pirates — Masters of Junks and Cunning Traps.

These pirates operated off the coasts of China, Vietnam, and the Philippines.
They used "junks" — special ships with sails that could turn even against the
wind. Their tactic was to lure into a trap: one ship appears, while others hide
behind an island. They also had "fire arrows" and even floating wooden mine
platforms. Sounds like a pirate ninja plan, right?

6. European Privateers — Pirates with Permission from Kings.

Privateers were pirates who had... a license! Yes, kings gave them permission
to attack enemy ships. For example, English privateers could plunder Spanish
galleons and even received a share of the loot. Their strategy was cunning and
surprise. They pretended to be neutral vessels, and then — boom! — boarded.
Some of them, like Francis Drake, became national heroes.

7. Vikings — Northern Pirates Who Could Do Everything: From Fighting to Farming.

Vikings were true masters of sea raids. Their "drakkar" ships had a shallow
draft, so they could enter rivers and attack from within the country! They
attacked quickly, without warning, and then disappeared before dawn. But
Vikings didn't just plunder — they also founded cities, built settlements, and
traded. And they even left magical runes on stones.

8. Why Does a Pirate Wear an Eye Patch? The Magic... of Darkness!

No, not all pirates were missing an eye! The eye patch was not just an
accessory, but a real life hack. A pirate could move from a bright deck to a dark
hold and see instantly. How? He kept one eye constantly in the dark under the
patch

When he needed to go below, he simply switched the patch to the other eye, and. . . saw in the dark! Super useful, right?

9. Secrets of the Crew: Signaling and Pirate Codes.

Pirates used clever signals: flags, whistles, bells, or even certain sail arrangements to signal each other. They had codes of conduct: for example, you couldn't steal from your mate, or else — no share of the treasure! The crew lived by rules that helped them survive, stay friendly, and always be ready for action.

10. Pirates — Not Just Swords and Cannons, but Strategists with a Capital S.

All these pirates, from the Caribbean to China, were not just hooligans with sabers. They knew how to think, plan, study maps, choose the right time, and even use psychology: they painted sails to scare the enemy or sang songs to seem carefree before an attack. True sea chess players!

Pirates are not just "Yo-ho-ho" and rum. They are strategists, travelers, inventors, and navigators. They knew how to fight, but even more — how to think. They knew that victory is not always about the sword, but sometimes about the mind. And also — that a crew, honor, and ginger tea can keep you afloat even in the stormiest times.

Printed in Dunstable, United Kingdom